Exploring the Secrets of the

Meadow-Thicket

Written by
JoAnne Dennee
and
Julia Hand

Illustrated by
Carolyn Peduzzi

Library of Congress Catalog Card Number: 93-74159

ISBN: 1-884430-02-3

Authors: JoAnne Dennee & Julia Hand

Editor: Jack Peduzzi

Illustrator: Carolyn Peduzzi

Book Design: Carolyn Peduzzi

We are grateful to the following people for their permission
to reprint or adapt their work: pg. 178, "Deep Deep",
author unknown, from *Children's Songs for a Friendly
Planet* by Evelyn Weiss, Children's Creative Response to
Conflict Resolution, Nyach, NY, © 1986; pg. 46, illustration, Carolyn Peduzzi; all other stories, poems and songs
are original work of the authors or Native American
legends retold through the oral tradition.

Printed on recycled paper

Exploring the Secrets of the
Meadow-Thicket

TABLE OF CONTENTS

Fall

Winter 🐾

Spring

Preface

For us at Food Works, and for literally hundreds of children, teachers, parents and community members, this Common Roots™ Guidebook represents far more than a collection of hands-on environmental activities for the young learner. For all of us, this Guide is a roadmap for placing schools back at the center of communities - by providing students with opportunities to address critical concerns in their neighborhoods, towns, surrounding countryside and larger world.

Food Works grew out of our community work attempting to unravel the spiral of hunger, poverty and ecological collapse locally and globally, from rural Vermont to urban centers.

Through this work, we discovered that the very ways we learn about the endangered world both reflect and recreate that world. In elementary school, for example, we learned to divide up the world into neat categories - Math, Science, Social Studies and so forth. We then applied those same tools in adulthood to divide up the world— Politics, Economics, Environment, etc.— which has led to a patchwork of temporary band-aids rather than sustainable solutions to these endemic problems.

In trying to create a world that nourishes all forms of life, we must from the earliest ages teach ourselves to see the world as an interconnected whole of which we are an integral part. We at Food Works believe the purpose of schooling should be to nurture the natural curiosity, imagination and dreams of all children, in order to re-create a world capable of responding to the diverse spectrum of intellectual, emotional, creative and nutritional needs of all its inhabitants.

Common Roots provides the practical skills enabling our children to more holistically understand and explore the inter-relationships between the natural and human world. Therefore, we at Food Works have dedicated our work to transform the role and responsibility of our schools in order to identify and respond to the food and ecological concerns of our communities in order to create a healthy future.

Joseph Kiefer

Acknowledgements

The *Common Roots*™ framework as a vehicle for re-inventing schools would not have been possible without the desire and enthusiasm of the many teachers, parents and children to change the way we look at the role of our schools.

The Rumney School was the first to offer us a school to pioneer the development of the *Common Roots* framework that included the K-6 Historic Theme Gardens.

The Barnet School hosted our first *Common Roots* graduate course which taught us the critical importance of each teacher owning his or her unique journey for integrated learning. This collaborative relationship continues to grow and bear fruit.

Additionally, we would like to thank all of our new schools and the unique way they have adopted *Common Roots* to meet their needs.

Unquestionably, none of this would have been possible without the dedication and vision of the Food Works collaborative team. The rich insights and personal teaching experiences of JoAnne Dennee, Julia Hand, Carolyn Peduzzi, Elisheva Kaufman, Jack Peduzzi, and Joseph Kiefer have inspired the genesis of *Common Roots*.

The guidance and support of our Board of Directors has been instrumental in sustaining the *Common Roots* vision. Their collective wisdom is a constant source of inspiration and direction.

Most importantly, we would like to acknowledge the many family and foundation funders whose generous support has enabled us to realize our common dream. By believing in our vision and continuing to support this evolving work, this group of friends has become part of our growing Food Works family.

Above all, listening to the voices of children has taught us the timely need to provide meaningful opportunities for them to create a better world.

A Word About *Common Roots*
A Guide to An Integrated, Living Curriculum

Welcome to the Common Roots Guidebooks, a collection of hands-on seasonal projects and activities for the curious child.

The Common Roots Guidebooks have been designed for teachers, parents and community members to create a living curriculum for children which integrates the human and ecological roots of their own community. These K-6 Guidebooks offer hands-on learning activities and projects for children to discover the past, explore the present and build their common future. These adventures are developmentally designed along a 7 year journey that help tell the story of each child's community, from its very first inhabitants (grades K-2) to its local heritage (grades 3-4) to a look to the future (grades 5-6), thereby creating a living curriculum of meaningful activities.

These Guidebooks integrate traditional subjects into each of the projects and activities that build upon each other as the child moves from Kindergarten through Sixth Grade. Social Studies is an integral part of the historic theme gardens - the hub of the Common Roots learning process for each grade level. The Applied Scientific Method is part of every activity. Children marvel at fermentation processes as they bake bread; track the life cycle of seeds; observe the effects of weather, fertilizer, insects and worms in their own gardens; and investigate and analyze sources of local water for pollution. Language arts are acquired as children write garden journals, read recipes or create a community ecology-action newsletter. Math skills are developed through designing a garden, measuring cooking ingredients and graphing changes in ecosystems. Art, music, dance and physical activity are also integrated into the activities to allow children to celebrate seasons and the cultures they are learning about.

Common Roots is an inquiry-based journey for children, guided by their teachers and parents and accompanied by their elders and neighbors. The meaningful hands-on projects and activities nurture children's natural curiosity by providing the opportunity for each child to express their creativity and knowledge in order to answer their own questions. This student-centered approach engages students in the process of learning rather than providing textbook answers to rigid curriculums.

Common Roots provides children with real-life opportunities to develop problem solving skills to research, document and help preserve their fragile environment and disappearing heritage - building a better world for

tomorrow. The projects and activities climax at the 6th Grade level, but the journey exploring our natural and human world is lifelong.

Put on your pack and come along with us!

INTRODUCTION TO THE MEADOW-THICKET GUIDEBOOK

In the Fall, when our story begins, the meadow-thicket is in its final preparations for the coming of Winter. Seeds are ripening, butterflies are migrating, animals are preparing their winter dens, and Grandforest Tree is standing tall at the edge of the forest, watching all that happens below him in the meadow-thicket.

Grandforest Tree and his friends guide children through the meadow-thicket on an adventure filled with stories, activities, and learning. The guidebook is divided into three sections, each representing the seasons of Fall, Winter, and Spring. Each section contains activities designed to slowly expand a child's knowledge of the meadow-thicket and to develop an understanding of the inter-relationships of all the meadow-thicket's inhabitants. As the seasons turn, the child's own place in the natural world also begins to unfold.

Each activity is based on a question or questions that *the child* asks, and then follows through with discoveries that lead to the answers. The activities are presented in such a way that one question leads to another. As well, within each activity is a section entitled "Want To Do More?", which guides the child to a deeper understanding of the world he or she is exploring. For the child who wishes to explore even further, another set of activities follows entitled "Even More Curious?" These activities include reading other suggested books or meeting with people who can elaborate upon the subject through their own life experiences.

Throughout the activities, traditional curricular studies are entwined. Thus, nature itself becomes the teacher of science, history, art, writing, music, and health. Frequently, a section entitled "Math, Nature's Way" is included in the activity. In this manner, the child receives an education that is relevant, engaging, and makes sense.

The delightful pen and ink illustrations that accompany each story invite color or paints. As you read a story, pass out a copy to each child. Afterwards, let them draw their own imaginative illustrations.

Should there be any questions, Grandforest Tree is always there to help.

FALL

Welcome To Fall

As the Autumn days grow shorter, the moon gains greater prominence in the sky. The sun sinks lower and lower on the horizon and the world grows colder and colder. The lush greens of summer turn to golds, reds, oranges, and yellows and finally to stark grey silhouettes outlined by the bluest of skies - or draped in the first snows of the year. Week by week, the seasonal rhythms of the Earth are revealed. Fall is a marvelous time of the year - especially in the Meadow-Thicket!

The sharp scent of leaves turning gold on the cool breeze makes it seem as if the meadow-thicket is coming to the end of its cycle. But, a careful look at cocoons tucked under curled leaves, at seeds spilling forth from dried plants that were once colorful flowers, and at whirling, swirling congregations of birds gathering to fly south, makes it seem as if the meadow-thicket is just beginning again. So many secrets of the meadow-thicket await your discovery!

Grandforest Tree stands tall and proud at the edge of the Meadow-Thicket, engaging children in projects and activities, delighting them with stories, and offering games to play. The Meadow-Thicket is a wonderful place to be in the Fall!

GOING WILD WITH EARS

EARS, the Ecology Action Research Station, is a gathering place for making discoveries and inquiries into the mysteries of the natural world. It can be located in any natural habitat such as a meadow-thicket, a pond, or a forest. Since this Guidebook will lead you through the wonders of the meadow-thicket, an EARS station should be established as close to a meadow-thicket as possible.

🐌 EARS can become a special place for visiting your meadow-thicket neighbors all year-round. EARS can be visited during weekly walks or hikes, for birthday celebrations, during full moons, beneath the light of the stars - even in your imagination! (During rainy weather, don't forget to bring your umbrellas!)

The EARS station can be anything you imagine it to be.

It can be a meadow or lawn area marked out by a circle of friends holding hands, or a circle of stones or stumps. It can be an area covered by a tarp or old tent fly, a rustic lean-to shelter covered with pine boughs, or a tipi-shaped shelter made of tree poles covered with branches and boughs, woven to create a screen. To make your lean-to or tipi waterproof, line it with recycled trash bags before covering it with boughs or branches.

🦌 **Tools** needed by the Ecology Action Researcher can be stored in the EARS station. These might include hand lens, magnifying boxes, insect sweeping nets, tracking cards, student-made identification necklaces, student journals, wildlife drawings that students have drawn and covered with contact paper, or web-of-life reference posters. All these research materials can be stored in hand-made field bags constructed of canvas, felt, leather, or any sturdy fabric. Tools can also be stored at the EARS station in waterproof containers or bins.

🦌 Walk around outdoors until you've found the special place you want to make your meadow-thicket EARS station. Sit down and see how your special place "feels". Think about the various ways you can construct or design your EARS station, then choose one that fits the special nature of your site. Be sure to make the station large enough to hold all of your friends. Now, think about the year stretching ahead, the unfolding secrets and mysteries of the meadow-thicket. Exciting adventures await you at your EARS station.

So, let's get started!

Adopt A
Nature Neighborhood

The meadow-thicket is full of life - a real Nature Neighborhood that you can adopt! Spend a season observing the successions and cycles in the meadow-thicket. Become its caretaker. You might enjoy building a temporary or permanent research shelter to house equipment. Seek shelter there during inclement weather. If no meadow area exists, you can actually create one!

Some suggestions follow.

🌿 First, with a group of friends or classmates, decide upon the area to adopt, such as a meadow-thicket with adjoining woods, or simply a nearby area of lawn.

🌿 Have everyone join hands in a circle to mark out the interior of this special nature area.

🌿 You can define the space with large stones or stumps, or weave a nature fence with limbs, yarn or fabric strips.

🌿 If the area is a lawn, leave it unmowed so it will become more meadow-like. You may need to get permission to keep it wild and free.

🌿 Make a trail through your adopted area, marking a path that meanders through the high grasses and shrubs. You can establish areas of interest along the way.

🌿 Try marking areas of interest with banners, such as a stencil of a flower or an ant, to entice people to stop and look around.

🔖 You can even give a name to your EARS habitat, such as "Wildflower Meadow" or "Secret Thicket".

🔖 Post a sign in your protected area, giving its name and the name of the person or persons who adopted it.

🔖 Come to an agreement regarding the use of your adopted place and the behaviors allowed around it. Write up these agreements and post them at your adopted place. After you have made your Meadow-Thicket Nature Journal, enter the agreements on the first page.

For example:

- ❂ Is picking or planting flowers permitted?
- ❂ Is it okay to walk or run inside the protected circle?
- ❂ Can a birdhouse be placed in the adopted meadow or thicket?
- ❂ May insects or tiny animals be removed from this adopted place?
- ❂ Will the peeling of bark or removal of live branches be permitted?

A DAY IN THE LIFE OF AN
ECOLOGY ACTION RESEARCHER

What can you do in your adopted forest or meadow-thicket? Explore!

Before heading out to your adoptive forest or meadow, consider the questions you hope to answer. Remember that the Ecology Action Researcher looks again and again and again - for more questions! Usually, the answers soon follow.

🐛 Look for small inhabitants as you poke around in the grasses.

🐛 Look for woodpecker holes in the bark. Can you find any insects living in them?

🐛 What kinds of plants dwell there?

🐛 Observe plant leaves. Are they flat, parallel to the ground? Long and slender? Toothed or lobed?

🐛 Look for signs of animal or insect life. Do you see scat (animal droppings)? Are there signs of plants being eaten? Can you find any tracks in the mud?

🐛 Choose one plant to observe. Get to know it well, just as you learn to know a friend by spending time together.

✍ Make a class diary, and keep it at your EARS station for recording the changes in your adopted meadow neighborhood. A three-ring binder that holds blank, unlined paper works well because you can refill it whenever necessary. The diary may contain rubbings, pressed flowers or illustrations. Poetry is a wonderful way to describe your observations. The class diary should be stored in a waterproof container to keep it safe and dry. Whenever anyone makes a great discovery, add it to the diary.

HOW DO I CARE FOR NATURE?
A NATURE NEIGHBORHOOD

Autumn provides many opportunities to observe the great harvest, as well as moments of peace in which to enjoy the beauty of the changing landscape. This is true even in urban settings.

     Can you plan a **Nature Neighborhood** project to show that you care for Nature? This project could be designed to attract wild creatures to your adopted meadow - or to your window sill. What is the best way to attract animals? By feeding them, of course!

     Any feature of the Nature Neighborhood you design can be arranged outside a nearby window, in the meadow-thicket, or around the Ecology Action Research Station. Here are some ideas to create and enhance your **Nature Neighborhood**:

     ● Fill bird or squirrel feeding stations with seeds collected from around the forest and meadow - such as pine cones, berries, hickory or beech nuts, thistle or sunflower seeds. Stuff a scarecrow-type character, put a tray filled with bird seed in his lap, then put the scarecrow outside the window. Hanging feeders can be placed in a tree or on window sills. Remember to fill the trays and feeders regularly with seeds.

     ● Place dried ears of corn outside for mice and squirrels. Even woodpeckers like them!

     ● You might also place some potted chrysanthemums in the Nature Neighborhood to feed butterflies and bees.

     ● To create a bird blind or fence around the Nature Neighborhood, weave a natural, native-style wall hanging. You can do this by warping a loom between two trees. This is easy to do - just wind string or yarn around and around two trees in a figure "8" fashion. Weave into the loom cattails, grasses, leaves, yarn, cloth strips, feathers, wildflowers - or anything else you can think of!

     ● Create a fence around the Nature Neighborhood, using two-foot long sticks decorated with dry ears of corn or sunflower heads. This will help define the special area you have set aside for your nature neighbors.

● Create an entrance to your Nature Neighborhood. Design a sign, and post it nearby. Enjoy the regular visits of friendly nature neighbors. Post a list of who visits - and what they do while there.

When your plans are complete, invite parents or community elders to help create your Nature Neighborhood.

🐦 How will you care for your Nature Neighborhood during the coming season? Share some of your observations about the ways in which Nature is caring for you.

Want To Do More?

🐦 What do you see, smell or feel during the harvest season? What are the ways in which Mother Earth is providing for you? Why do you think some people call this time of year the "great give-away"?

🐦 Make a mural showing how Mother Earth cares for us, and how we care for her, during the season of the great give-away. There are many ways to show how we care for Nature. Use your imagination!

CREATE YOUR OWN
NATURE NEIGHBORHOOD JOURNAL

Each observer of the meadow-thicket can make her very own journal. It can contain observations, drawings, poems, thoughts and reflections.

A 3-ring binder works well as a journal. A more creative version can be made by using yarn to "sew" the paper between the poster board covers. The journal should have enough blank pages to last an entire season.

🐌 As you observe the meadow-thicket Nature Neighborhood, **write down any questions** that arise. During the next "re-search" session, look for answers to these questions. More questions for the Ecology Action Researcher are sure to follow! Repeat this activity throughout the seasons to gain a sense of the rhythm of the landscape.

✍ **Illustrate** animal scat, tracks, or any interesting thing you find.

✍ **Record** the types of plants that have been eaten. Also, record the markings made on plants by browsing animals - such as teeth marks, holes or bites in the plant. The height of the marks may provide clues as to the type of animal that did the browsing.

✍ Record **Haiku poetry** in your nature journal. Haiku is a type of poetry especially suited for nature observations. Haiku has no rhyme, and is usually three lines long. The first line has five syllables, the second line seven syllables, and the last line five syllables. For example:

Early in the morn
The Earth sighs a gentle breath
And I grow a smile.

NATURE NAMES:
BIRCH BARK EMBLEMS

Native people and the clans they belong to are often given the name of animals, plants or elements. This demonstrates their relationship to others in the family circle of life. Iroquois clans include the Bear Clan, Wolf Clan, Beaver Clan and Heron Clan. Perhaps you would like to choose a nature name that expresses your special connection to a particular plant, animal or element.

The following guided journey can assist you in preparing the way for finding a nature name.

Find a comfortable place so you can settle into your imagination and find your nature sister or brother. Close your eyes, take a few deep breaths. . . and get ready to begin.

"Imagine yourself on a nature hike, going to a favorite place where you can be at one with the Earth. Feel the sun or shadows on your body. Look around at the colors, smell the scents of nature, feel the peacefulness of the place. Look! - a small entrance in the landscape invites you. You step into the opening, moving as though in a dream down a dark but peaceful corridor. Before long you come out the other side of the opening - it is as if you have passed through a tunnel to another world!

"Ah, you have come to the land where all Nature dwells. What beauty! Look around for a moment at all the splendor. What do you see here?

"Wait! Soon you shall be greeted by your special nature friend. Listen! Someone speaks, not with the familiar voice of a human, but with the voice of nature: 'Welcome, Nature's Friend, to this land where all nature lives in harmony.' Look around, for the face of your nature brother or sister is among all that you see here. Your nature friend may reach out to touch you, to greet you in its own special way. Do not be afraid. Is it wing, paw, fin, branch or flower that touches you? Return the gesture of friendship by placing your hand upon your nature brother or sister.

"What do you feel and see? Are there ways that you and your nature friend are alike? Just for a moment, you may begin to look and feel exactly like your nature friend! Take a few minutes to enjoy these magical moments. Your nature friend touches you again, this time in farewell, then reaches out to give you a gift. Accept this treasure as you say farewell.

"Now your journey back to your world begins. Return along the peaceful corridor. When you arrive back where you started, rest quietly. Daydream about your nature friend, and think about the meaning of the gift you were given."

ዿ If you went on a guided journey with several friends, now is a good time to have a share circle to tell what happened to you. What was the special gift you received? What does it mean to you?

ዿ Take a nature name from your nature friend. You might like to share this name with friends who appreciate adventures in the natural world.

ዿ In what ways are you and your nature friend the same? Different? In order to survive, are there things that you share in common?

Want To Do More?

ዿ Create a birch bark emblem that illustrates your nature friend and its name, and keep it close to your heart.

A Birch Bark Emblem

You will need:

a 6" square of birch bark
a willow branch, at least 24" long
pencils, crayons, or markers
yarn or waxed linen

1) Cut a 4" circle or oval from a section of fallen birch bark. With a leather punch or hole punch, carefully punch holes around the outside edges of the birch bark circle. Illustrate the birch bark with colored pencils, crayons or markers. Watercolors work well, too.

2) With a length of soaked willow, make a circular hoop slightly larger than the birch bark circle. Bind the willow hoop together with waxed linen, or yarn, to represent the sinew used by Native people long ago.

3) Next, place the birch bark inside the willow hoop. Using the waxed linen or yarn, loosely lace the birch bark circle inside the willow hoop. Make a braid from three pieces of the linen or yarn. Fasten both ends of the braid at the top of the emblem. Make sure that the braid is long enough so that, when worn around your neck, the emblem hangs near your heart.

Many Native people wear near their heart a totem that helps keep them in "balance". It reminds them that the power of these objects keeps them vital - full of health, strength and well-being in body, mind and heart. These objects are often referred to by Native peoples as their "medicine", and are treated with great respect. What lessons, or medicine, might your nature friend share with you that will help you grow in body, mind and spirit?

(continued)

In Native cultures, animals have great significance. All animals have power because the essence of the Great Spirit is believed to dwell within them, as well as within rocks and plants. The names of Native people often refer to a part of nature that becomes an ally. Their animal helper or friend links them to the Great Spirit, giving them power. Their friend tells them stories, and often appears to them in dreams. Strength comes from these teachings, and the person is instructed to live up to them.

For example, Turtle brings good "medicine power" - the healing life force - to others. She transports her charges on her back, carrying her own home wherever she goes. Some Native people believe she even carries the world upon her back. This takes a great deal of strength and endurance. Did you know that Turtle's heart beats for three days after Turtle dies? This is why Native peoples believe that Turtle's "medicine" gives one strength and a strong heart.

Often, Native people befriend the nature friend that represents the quality or challenge they are working on in their life. The beaver represents industry, the deer gentleness, the butterfly an ability for great change and lightheartedness, the chipmunk the need to provide comfort for oneself. The nature friend may become an ally for learning whatever lesson is needed at the time. Native people view this as a special opportunity to work with their nature friend on a real-life journey.

Over time, reflect upon lessons, poems or imaginative adventure stories with your nature friend by doing some **creative writing** in your journal. If you wish, share some of these teachings and discoveries with a friend.

Even More Curious?

Do you want to work with your nature friend on a life challenge? **Read** some Native American legends or animal fables about your new nature friend. Or, quietly **observe** your nature animal friend to see what it can teach you.

LUNAR CALENDARS

One way to become more conscious of the natural patterns and cycles of the land is to observe and record seasonal rhythms. A Native Lunar Calendar is helpful for recording observations and documenting the rhythms of the Earth through each changing season. This calendar can become a useful reference for predicting weather phenomena or for comparing how patterns vary within a state, region or country. Display the calendar indoors or at the Ecology Action Research Station.

The calendars we use today have shifted from lunar measurements to a different system. How are they different? Observe the moon and record its phases for a period of at least one month.

🐚 What do you notice about lunar rhythms?

🐚 How long is a lunar cycle?

🐚 What measurement is used in our present monthly cycle?

🐚 Is our current calendar based on lunar rhythms or another rhythm?

Native Lunar Calendar

Many Native American peoples follow a calendar based on annual moon cycles. One complete moon cycle (28 days) measures these periods. Each lunar period was given a name that honored its special characteristics. Of course, Native calendar names differed according to the habitat and geography of each nation. For example, Vermont Abenakis named their moons after activities or events that occurred during each moon. Can you guess which months go with the following names? New Year's Greeting Moon, Shedding Boughs Moon, Moose Hunting Moon, Sugar Making Moon, Planting Moon, Hoeing Moon, Hay Making Moon, Harvest Moon, Indian Corn Reaping Moon, Falling Leaf Moon, Ice-Forming Moon.

🐚 If you were to name the months or moons according to natural phenomena or the activities you participate in, what would those names be?

(continued)

✍ Record your observations of each season in a journal or on a calendar.

🐦 List some of the changes you observe as the Earth's relationship to the Sun changes during these times of the year.

🐦 Illustrations may be helpful for remembering new discoveries.

FLOWER PRESSES

Wouldn't it be wonderful if you could save the flowers of summer and fall forever? You can! Just make a simple flower press and you will be able to preserve all the beautiful flowers of the meadow-thicket.

A pocket-size **flower press** is just the right size to carry on the trail. It can be made from recycled materials.

A Flower Press

You will need:

Corrugated cardboard for the outer cover
Several thin pieces of cardboard
Newsprint or manila paper
2 strong rubber bands
Markers, paints, crayon or nature magazine photos
A little glue
Clear Contact paper (optional)

1) Cut two pieces of thick corrugated cardboard approximately 4 x 6 inches

2) Decorate the outsides of the cardboard with paint, marker, crayon, magazine clippings, dried flower or recycled wrapping paper

3) Cover the cardboard with clear Contact paper for added protection.

4) Put your name inside.

5) Fold five pieces of 8 x 6 inch manila paper in half so that they measure 4 x 6 inches.

6) Sandwich each batch of folded manila papers inside thin, 8 x 6 inch cardboard that has been folded to 4 x 6 inches, and finish by sandwiching these between thick cardboard covers.

7) Wrap the finished press with rubber bands.

❧ Take this pocket size press along on the EARS Trail or any

nature hike. Gather small flowers that will fit inside the press. Place specimens carefully inside the manila pages. When you are finished collecting, wrap the press securely with rubber bands to put a little pressure on it. Allow a week or two to dry the specimens. If you need to have them finished sooner than that, press them for one day, then iron the specimens between paper with an iron set on "permanent press". Press with the iron for a minute or two, depending on the thickness and moisture content of the blossom or leaf.

> ☛ **Note:** *Only pick from areas where flowers are abundant. Avoid areas where it looks as if the flowers have already been harvested. It is important to leave untouched at least 2/3 of the flowers of each species. This will ensure a good seed crop for next year's flowers, as well as ensuring that other people are able to enjoy these colorful friends.*

🌰 Create homemade flower identification guides. Be sure to Identify the flowers before pressing them, as the color and shape often change slightly during drying. You might also enjoy making greeting cards or other flower art projects. A flower press can be enjoyed over and over again!

🌰 Save pressed flowers and plants throughout the seasons. Create a poster of Flower and Plant Neighbors in your meadow-thicket neighborhood.

Flower Math, Nature's Way

1) Gather in small groups or pairs and collect flowers in a field or meadow where there is an abundance of specimens. (Remember to leave at least 1/3 of the flowers in each cluster.) Carefully place the flowers in recycled plastic or paper bags.

2) When your group has finished collecting flowers, sit down in a place where the flowers won't blow away and where you can spread out. Sort and classify the flowers into categories that make sense to your group.

3) After sorting the flowers, choose someone to speak for the group, explaining why you chose to organize the flowers as you did.

For an exciting challenge, count how many flowers you have in each category, then make a bar graph from this information.

"THE BUTTERFLY TREE"

Grandforest Tree remembers the night of the monarchs:

Once, years ago, a huge flock of black- white- and yellow-striped monarch butterflies visited me on their way South. It was early Fall, and my leaves were just beginning to turn. I had been feeling very sad because the human family who had been living here for three generations had moved away. There were no cows seeking my cool shade, no children climbing into my branches or playing on the tire swing.

"It had been a rainy, warm Summer, and insects - particularly mosquitoes, butterflies and moths - had been especially abundant. As the days shortened and the nights cooled, flocks of geese could be heard heading South. Other birds, as well, gathered and flew to warmer climates. Crickets made music in the meadow-thicket, cheerfully chirping in the still green grasses.

"One evening, just as the sun was about to set behind the ridge, a couple of butterflies landed on my top-most leaves. Suddenly there were several, then hundreds, then thousands of monarchs surrounding me, beating their black- white- and yellow-striped wings in a flurry of excitement. One by one, they slowly settled, covering my every leaf and twig! Instead of a Maple tree, I was a monarch tree!

"After a few minutes of restlessness, the flock quieted down. Then a thin, tired voice spoke: 'Hello, Mister Maple tree! Pardon our intrusion, but we had to land somewhere for the night. A storm is coming and the upper winds are very rough. We were afraid we might be blown off course! So we came down to see if we could find a place to rest, and you looked like a wonderful sleeping spot. Your leaves make the most divine pillows, by the way.'

"Well, the little fellow chatted on and on despite the fact that he was quite exhausted from his journey. After awhile they all began to chime in - it was quite a din! High, babbling butterfly voices, all talking at once! I guess they don't get to exercise their voices when they are flying. It didn't last long, however - most of them fell asleep talking.

"Sure enough, a violent storm swept through the meadow-thicket that night, wrestling with my leaves and branches. But do you know what? Those monarchs held tight and hardly any of them fell off! When the sun came out early the next morning, they opened and closed their wings in grateful greeting. Then, by twos, then fours, then tens, then hundreds, they took off, flying high into the rain-washed sky, bidding me farewell in their high-pitched, sing-songy voices. They circled the meadow three times, and continued on their journey South.

"That was an unforgettable experience. It taught me that miracles can happen even when things look bleak and dreary.

"But I'm not the only one who remembers the experience. Once in awhile, a young monarch or monarch caterpillar will drop by to tell me that his great-great-great-great-great-great-great grandmother spent the night among my leaves, where she rode out a violent storm. Perhaps one day I will host another exhausted flock of butterflies.

"And if you are lucky, maybe the monarchs will visit your meadow-thicket on their way South. Keep a watchful eye this fall for a flock of monarchs!"

MONARCH MIGRATION: MAKE A TERRARIUM

Early September is a good time for gathering insects in the meadow. If you want to observe the fascinating process of insect metamorphosis, look for a monarch caterpillar or chrysalis to put in a terrarium. It will turn into a butterfly before your eyes!

🐛 Look daily for black- white- and yellow-striped monarch caterpillars. You can find them in the meadow, especially on Milkweed plants, which are their main food staple.

🐛 When you find one, make a list of questions in your journal. Search carefully for any interesting adaptations. Can you differentiate between the front and the rear of the monarch caterpillar? Monarch caterpillars are known for an extra set of horn-like antennae. You may notice the worm waving these black, horn-like objects at you! Why do you think they do this?

To make a caterpillar terrarium

You will need:

a large glass jar
moss
rocks
milkweed plants
meadow flowers
a bare branch
a small vase to fit inside the jar

1) Find a large, reusable glass jar.

2) Cover the bottom with moss and rocks. Oftentimes, someone will put a lonely caterpillar in a stark container. But there is no reason to do this. It is simple to provide some of Mother Nature's environment for the monarch caterpillar.

3) Provide an ample food supply for caterpillars by placing a small vase of milkweed plants and other meadow flowers in the terrarium. Caterpillars eat milkweed, but butterflies emerging from the chrysalis love nectar. A few blossoms of autumn flowers, such as wild asters, will do. As caretakers, please remember daily to replenish the milkweed or aster supply.

4) Place a bare branch in the terrarium for caterpillars to crawl upon as they spin their chrysalis.

5) Cover the terrarium with a piece of sheer fabric, or punch holes in the jar's lid so the insects can breathe.

6) Clean the terrarium of excessive caterpillar droppings.

7) In fourteen days, expect a miracle! That's about how long it takes for a caterpillar to spin its chrysalis and emerge as a butterfly.

You are not disturbing the caterpillar's normal life cycle by placing it in the terrarium so long as you provide food and room for it to forage and to spin a chrysalis. If you wish to maintain the caterpillar's normal environment, keep the terrarium outdoors, but remember to keep it sheltered from the rain. You can also bring your terrarium indoors at this time of year, as the inner and outer environments are nearly the same. If you keep your terrarium out of direct sunlight, it will not become overheated.

Want To Do More?

As you discover some mysteries of the Monarch, you can:

🐛 **Record and illustrate daily observations** of caterpillar, chrysalis, and butterfly activities in your nature journal.

🐛 **Research and describe stages of insect metamorphosis.** You can draw a cartoon or make some papier mache models to demonstrate what you learn. For a papier mache exhibit, make an egg, caterpillar, and chrysalis. A fully grown butterfly, complete with fabric or tissue paper and pipe cleaner wings, is really neat!

🐛 **Supply a meal of nourishing nectar** after the butterfly emerges. Place wild asters in the terrarium, or put in wadded paper towels that are saturated with sugar water (to do this, dissolve two teaspoons of sugar in a cup of water and pour into the wadded paper towels). Do not be alarmed if your butterfly does not eat after emerging, but notice whether its "proboscis" begins to move.

A proboscis is a long, tube-like straw which curls and uncurls as the butterfly probes for nectar. Butterflies smell with their feet to determine what is food. Some butterflies eat very little as their main purpose in life is to lay eggs for the next generation, so they are not very hungry. Observe the feeding behaviors of

your monarch before releasing it. After the butterfly pumps its wings to dry them, and has had 12 hours of recovery time, you can set it free. Plan a release celebration.

❧ **Wondering where your monarch might go** upon release may inspire you to do some reading about monarch migration. You might discover some incredible monarch mysteries! Record these fascinating discoveries in your nature journal, or make a puppet show and demonstrate the wonders of the butterfly world.

❧ **Discover how butterflies find their way South** during migration. Can you orient yourself to the South using landmarks, the sun, a compass or a map? Place a large paper monarch on the southern wall of your room to remind yourself which way is South. Can you find North? East? West? See if you can learn other interesting facts about monarchs, such as where they go when migrating. How far do they fly? How long does it take them to get there? How many miles do they fly each day?

❧ **Perform a simple puppet show** that demonstrates the development of the butterfly from egg to adult. Perhaps the puppets can tell a story about a caterpillar who anxiously awaits the long flight South. Unexpectedly, a small boy picks him up and brings him indoors. What happens to the caterpillar's longing to fly?

To make a stage for the puppet theater, drape a cloth over a table. Embellish the theater with moss, flowers, green cloth (for a meadow), some stones and sticks. A butterfly's body can be made from a stick, its wings from doubled shades of tissue paper. A puppeteer's handle can be made by looping thread to both ends of the stick. A gentle up and down motion allows the wings to flap.

❧ **Make up a story** about a butterfly journeying from your yard southward to Mexico.

(continued)

Even More Curious?

❧ **Consider how we, like butterflies, grow and change.** Write a storybook, complete with photos, about your own changing life.

❧ **Create a meadow food web** that demonstrates the role of the monarch caterpillar and butterfly.

Math, Nature's Way

❧ Make up addition and subtraction word problems that involve butterflies. Give these problems to your friends and challenge them to solve them.

For example, if ten butterflies are fluttering across a meadow, and a young boy captures five in his butterfly net, how many are left? Or, if two butterflies are swept by the wind across your front lawn, and then two more butterflies are swept along on the same breeze, how many butterflies are caught in the breeze? Can you think of other examples?

"BUTTERFLY"

From a single, smooth white oval egg
emerged a curious caterpillar.
Black and white and yellow-streaked,
with a short snout
and stout stubby legs.
He was quite magnificent.
Two antennae waved in the air,
searching for food, and found it -
right beneath his pudgy feet.
He began to eat and eat and eat,
gorging several leaves in several hours
nonstop for several days.
Then he fastened his hindmost feet
securely with silk
and hung up-side down
from an especially juicy milkweed leaf.
As by magic, his squat, striped body
became
a shiny-green, gold-speckled
chrysalis.
Our fat friend was in a deep, dreamy sleep, dreaming
of flying freely over the milkweed-filled meadow.
And while he slept and dreamt,
his strange pudgy body began to change
into something quite fine.
Once more he emerged
bedraggled, but dressed his best -
firey-orange wings, sleek, streamlined body,
delicate antennae, and black, skinny legs.
Soon he spread his sun-dried wings
and flew over the milkweed
in search of friends
to fly south with.

J.H.

Seeds in the Meadow - Thicket

At the end of September, many Native Americans gather seeds for next year's crop. Now is a good time for you to hike to a garden or meadow to find seeds for next year's growing project.

❦ As you go on a meadow hike or walk into a garden, seeds will disperse from their parent plants and attach themselves to your socks. A fun way to deal with this picky dilemma is to wear an old pair of socks over your shoes! When you finish your **seed sock walk**, take some time to discover how each little seed found a way to hitchhike or travel on you. When you return to the classroom, sort the seeds by species into egg cartons. How is each seed's method of hitch hiking different?

❦ Determine the parent plant for each seed you found. On your next trip to the meadow, look for parent plants cradling young seeds.

❦ How does each plant family carry seeds? Record your findings in your **nature journal**. Laminate seeds and parent plant leaf pressings alongside drawings of the parent plant in your journal. Clear Contact paper, waxed paper or glue works well as a laminate. If you don't know the name of a plant or seed, try naming it according to its characteristics. Research its name later, using a wildflower identification guide.

Want To Do More?

❦ **Save seeds from your sock walk to sow a wildflower garden** next year. Seeds from nature will require a period of chilling in the refrigerator. This mimicking of Winter will encourage flowers to "sleep", or become dormant. The following Spring, germinate the meadow seeds indoors. Can you name the meadow plants as they emerge?

🐛 **Design an art project** using felt and the seeds that hitchhiked on you. Do some of the seeds resemble nature's velcro? Seeds can be arranged as mosaics, shaped into burr baskets or other sculptures, or used to depict an Autumn nature scene. It's fun to identify the names of seeds. Arrange seeds by groups, then spell out their names on a flannel board.

🐛 September 27th is American Indian Day. You might want to plan an event that **commemorates the Native people** who have passed down seeds from generation to generation. Don't forget, this is also the best time of year to gather and trade seeds!

Math, Nature's Way

🍎 Sort and classify seeds into egg cartons. Count the number of seeds in each group, then make a bar graph to display the information.

"HOME AGAIN, HOME AGAIN"

Grandforest Tree conveys a warning about collecting meadow-thicket friends:

L et me tell you a story about a grasshopper friend of mine named Hooper, who lived in the meadow-thicket one hot, dry Summer. He was a happy fellow. Often I would hear him down there in the grass that grew about my roots, singing with a chorus of other late summer insects.

"But there was a time when Hooper was very upset indeed. For he had been through a traumatic adventure, having been trapped in a glass jar for two days with nothing but a few blades of grass to eat and no one to talk to.

"He said he would always remember how hot and stuffy it was in the jar, which had been left forgotten in the hot August sun. Finally Hooper was released. But to make matters worse, he was dumped without care into an unfamiliar meadow!

"After he recovered from this near-death experience, Hooper climbed a a tall blade of grass to get his bearings. To his dismay, he did not recognize a single tree, bush or rock! Where was the huge Grandfather Maple in the middle of the field? Where was the familiar rock wall that flanked the west end of the meadow-thicket, separating it from the forest? Where were all his brothers and sisters, his parents, cousins, aunts and uncles? What had happened to all his friends?

"Hooper listened carefully to the singing of other

grasshoppers who rubbed their back legs together in the afternoon heat. He understood what they were saying, but he did not recognize a single voice! Sadly, he hopped onto a flat, black boulder to get a better look. The landscape was unfamiliar in all directions. 'Oh dear, how will I ever get home!' Hooper sniffed, his teardrops splattering on the rock.

'Sssssssss. . . pppaaarrrdonnn mee, buttt arrrre you losssssssst?' hissed a beautiful, long Garter snake who sunned himself on the rock.

"Hooper was so startled he almost jumped off the rock. 'Oh, I can't tell you how sorry I am - I didn't mean to disturb you. Yes, I am very lost!' Hooper then told the snake of his miserable escapade in the jar, and how he had been dumped far from his home and family. Amazingly, the snake was undergoing a similar experience, and the two of them began to commiserate.

"Unbeknownst to them, a wise old Goshawk surveyed the rock from a nearby tree. Goshawks are quite fond of snakes - they especially like to eat them as late afternoon appetizers. However, the Goshawk had just finished a very large meal and was not hungry. But she was interested in their conversation, for her own brother had been taken from the nest by a human who wanted a pet, and the Goshawk had never forgotten it. Moreover, she had quite a reputation for being unfriendly and fierce, and as a result had few friends. Hoping to change this image and make new friends, she decided to help the two creatures that chatted on the flat, black rock.

"Goshawk flew to the grass at the foot of the rock. In her kindest voice she introduced herself, explaining that she was lonely and wished to change her ferocious ways.

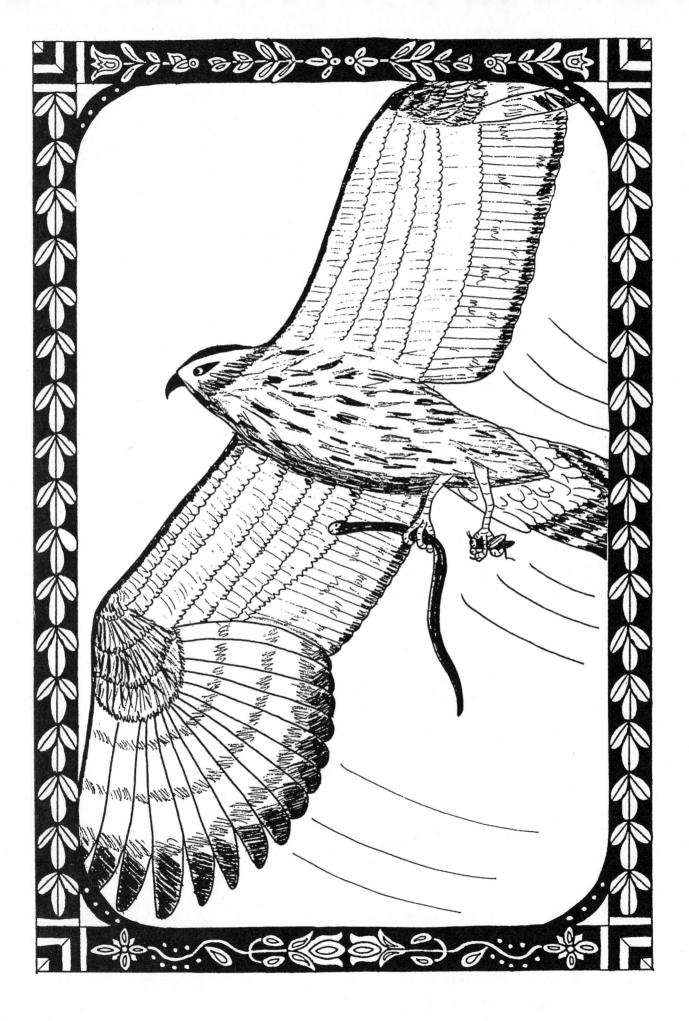

Then she told them her plan. 'If you trust me to carry you gently in my claws, I think I can find your meadow-thicket. It sounds like one I have visited many times to catch mice.'

"Hooper was immediately interested. The snake, however, was understandably wary - Goshawks are a snake's most dangerous enemy. But the mouse population in the field where he currently lived was dwindling, and he longed for better hunting. Eventually, he agreed to go along.

"Very gently, the Goshawk scooped up Hooper and the Garter snake in her sharp claws. She flapped her wings - and they were off!

"Up, up, and over the field the three of them soared. They flew over a road, another field, some houses, a large pond and a forest. Soon the Goshawk began to circle a field filled with blackberry bushes. Below her there were also some young trees, lots of long scraggly grass, and, in the middle of the field, a huge old Maple tree. 'That's it! That's my home!' chirped Hooper.

"'Yessss,' hissed the snake, 'miiine toooo!'

"Landing on the old stone wall, the Goshawk unclenched her claws, releasing Hooper and the snake. They were both very excited to be home again. 'How can we ever thank you?' sang Hooper.

"'Yessss,' hissed the snake, 'there musssst be sssssssomething we can dooo.'

"'Your gratitude is more than enough,' the Goshawk said. 'I am tired of being friendless and fierce. It's nice to know I have some friends who can trust me.' With that she flew off into the evening sky, returning to her home.

"Well, Hooper was thrilled to return to the meadow! For days afterwards he perched in the grass growing about my roots, singing and singing. But he never forgot the traumatic adventure, and often spoke of it.

"So remember - if <u>you</u> catch something in the meadow-thicket, take good care of it. Make sure the little creature has plenty of food, keep it out of direct sunlight, and gently put it back in the same place you found it!"

MEADOW SWEEPING STATION

Have you ever heard the loud buzz, chirp, and chirree of the meadow-thicket at night? Do you wonder who's making all that noise? Meadow sweeping gently collects many of these talkative friends so you may become acquainted with them.

For this activity, everyone should stroll out into the high grasses of the meadow-thicket, or visit an unmowed area of lawn. "Sweep it" for a close up look at meadow inhabitants.

You will need:

several butterfly nets or
large sheets of sheer fabric
insect boxes
magnifying lens or
viewing boxes

❧ If you have butterfly nets, use them in a gentle sweeping motion through the tall grasses. After a minute of sweeping, gently close the end of the net, then look into it. You'll be amazed at what you'll find inside! Which ones crawl? Which fly? Which jump?

❧ When observing meadow inhabitants with a large group, put a tent made of netting over an area and observe the insect critters within. For a better view of the more interesting critters, gently place them in a large magnifying box.

🐦 A few minutes of observation should reveal information about body parts, movement, mouth parts, unique characteristics, and diet. When you set your nature neighbor free, follow it, observing the way it moves and where it goes. Can you locate the types of plants it prefers for shelter or food?

Nature journals can contain exciting observations, such as:

- Drawings of the meadow neighbor.
- A list of your questions.
- Illustrations of all the body parts. Why are the parts special? What do they do?
- Descriptions of how your meadow neighbor travels through the meadow.

Don't forget to swap journals and share your findings with a friend!

🐦 Each time you go to the meadow or lawn, you might find new insect neighbors. If you don't know their names, try to name them according to their special qualities or characteristics. When you return to your classroom, identify them with the help of a special book called a "key". Using a key is somewhat like using a dictionary, and is an important tool to master. You might enjoy making your own "Key to Insects in the Meadow-Thicket".

GRASSHOPPER'S JOURNEY

Stalking a grasshopper or any six-legged insect is one of the best ways to learn about the world of insects! This might sound easy, but you may discover that insects have remarkable adaptations that enable them to journey through the world of the meadow more easily than you.

Try this challenge! **Can you follow a grasshopper for ten minutes?** To stay on the trail of this six-legged, you might enjoy working in pairs or with a small group of friends. Before you begin stalking the insect, you might want to write any **questions** you have about grasshoppers in your journal.

You will need:

a grasshopper
viewing box (optional)
drawing materials
cardboard
paint
brass fasteners

🐛 **Observe** a grasshopper for ten minutes. How does the insect move? Does it waddle or creep along? Does it take slow, steady steps? Is it a long leaper? Or does it flip-flap soar, traveling by wing?

🐛 Take time to **observe the six-legged friend as it eats**. Notice how the mouth parts are perfectly adapted for food gathering. What else do you see? What does it eat and how does it do it? Are the mouth parts designed to chew or suck? Enter these observations into your nature journals.

🐛 **What colors the world of a grasshopper?** Take a look into the world of the insect. What do you see when you look closely at it? How do insects see their world? Place a grasshopper in a large magnifying box for a few minutes. Look for your insect friend's eye parts. Do you see a tiny, bead-like eye on the front of its head? This eye is similar to a magnifying lens for seeing things up close. Now look for large compound eyes that help the insect to see distant objects.

How many compound eyes are there? How are these eyes adapted for the world of insects? Even with both sets of eyes, insects cannot see well. How do you think insects find their homes, food, or their enemies?

🐛 You might enjoy this **art activity to demonstrate the visual world of insects**. Using colored pastels on white paper, draw a picture of the way you think an insect sees its world - meadow flowers looming overhead, perhaps. With a tissue, smudge or gently rub the completed drawing. This blurry but beautiful insect world might make a nice display alongside illustrations of insect friends. Create a story about the journey taken together.

🐛 Imitate insect movement patterns in a game of **Six-Legged Charades**. First, practice the movements. Try to imitate the flip - flap. . float-t-t-t-t of a butterfly. Or try the grasshopper's leap - leap. . . soar-r-r-r-r. . . rest! Why do you think the insect needs to move in its particular way? Does its movement help it to avoid other insects or objects? How far can it move in a single step or flap of a wing? Take some time to discover these amazing insect adaptations!

🐛 Make a **giant 2-D model of grasshopper adaptations**. Cut out cardboard body parts. Show mouth parts, compound eyes, jointed legs, and wing covers. Pierce the moving body parts with brass clips, then fold the clip's fasteners to secure the moving pieces. Demonstrate adaptations!

SIX- AND EIGHT - LEGGEDS IN THE MEADOW - THICKET

Investigate the nearly invisible life of a meadow-thicket by observing the intricacies of the six-leggeds who reside there. This can be done by quietly observing these creatures with a hand lens, by stalking and gently catching them, or by designing an observation house in the EARS shelter for more extended care and study. Soon you will be able to recognize and demonstrate the difference between insects and spiders, as well as explain their important role in the food cycle of the meadow-thicket.

Imagine you are passing through an incredible shrinking machine that reduces you to the size of an ant or some other insect! Notice how differently things appear to you as you enter into the world of the six- and more-leggeds. Grass towers over your head. Pebbles have become boulders. Flowers look like gigantic trees stretching into the sky. What is it like to travel from one place to another? What obstacles do you encounter?

&⬤ Before beginning your journey into the incredible shrinking machine, you might want to:

⬤ List all the questions you want answered while in the miniature world of insects.

&⬤ After returning from your journey, you may want to:

⬤ Illustrate body parts of different insects (or non-insects) you observed. It might be helpful temporarily to put a meadow neighbor in a magnifying box so you can observe and sketch details. As soon as you can, release your neighborly neighbor with a "Thanks!"

⬤ Tell a story about the roles of the six- and eight-leggeds in their society, as well as their role in yours. Describe the process of food acquisition and distribution that you observed.

✍ Record your observations about insects in your nature journal.

How do you feel being reduced to a small size? Does size have any relationship to the value you add to the world?

Want To Do More?

🐌 You might enjoy **designing an insect costume** that displays all the fascinating details of a six- or eight-legged meadow neighbor. It could be just the thing for Halloween this year! Here are some suggestions for making a cricket costume.

1) Design a black helmet from paper plates. Attach long antennae to it.

2) Wear a painted box for the thorax. Allow pairs of jointed legs to dangle from the box. One pair of legs may be represented by real arms, complete with pincers for food gathering. Another pair of legs can be your own legs. The middle pair could hang from the thorax box. Make wings that project from the back of the thorax box.

3) If you decide to use your own body parts for legs, then an abdomen can be added to the rear of the thorax box.

For a tasty snack, carry along some mature grasses. You'll get hungry after all that leaping and chirping!

"Celia's Jewels"

Grandforest Tree explains why spiders' webs are so dazzling :

Celia was a beautiful, long-legged spider with a tan body and great beady eyes that stuck out from the top of her head. She lived in the grasses of the meadow-thicket long ago, when it was a field newly settled by the farmer and his family.

"I remember when Celia first introduced herself to me. It was a warm summer afternoon, and the shadows were beginning to lengthen across the greening field when she gently touched my bark with her skinny spider legs. I was just a youthful sapling then, about seven years old and perhaps five feet tall, but she seemed very small when I gazed down at her with a questioning look.

"She told me her name was Celia, and explained that she was looking for a suitable place to build her web. She asked if it would be okay if she climbed upon my trunk to have a better look at the meadow. I welcomed her, telling her to crawl on up and seek shelter beneath one of my leaves, as the day was growing late.

"Celia ambled up my trunk to have a look about the meadow. After a minute or two she spied a number of potential web sights, but instead of climbing down she sought shelter beneath one of my leaves, accepting my offer to sleep there. Before dozing off she told me about her life as a spider, weaving webs and trapping flies. I described my comparatively sedentary life as a tree, telling her how I loved to watch the meadow change during the cycles of the year. After awhile her eyes drooped, and she slept soundly.

"As the dawn sky began to lighten, she crept quietly down my trunk. I watched her crawl among the grasses to a thatch of timothy growing near the rock wall. She

immediately began to weave an intricate, perfect pattern across two stems of grass - a web to ensnare unwary flies. Her work was done in about an hour. Then she sat down to wait for a juicy meal. Before she was able to trap a fly, however, the farmer walked into her web on his way to fix a hole in the rock wall. Poor Celia. She had to start all over again. When she was almost finished, two of the farmer's children, playing innocently in the grass, destroyed the web. Undaunted by the seemingly endless task, Celia again repaired her web. Eventually she was successful, catching a fat fly for dinner!

"During the weeks that followed, I watched Celia's struggles. Often she fixed her web several times in a single day. But she never complained, no matter how tired she became.

"One morning, the fairy Goddess of the Grasses became entangled in the web. Celia, thinking she had caught her breakfast, stopped short of sinking her fangs into the little fairy's body. 'Oh my,' said Celia, 'you're not a fly at all! You look much too pretty to eat.'

"Despite her hunger, Celia carefully cut away the sticky bonds that trapped the fairy Goddess of the Grasses. 'Why thank you, Celia,' said the grateful fairy. 'I didn't see your web at all.' She stared at the huge hole Celia had to repair. 'I'm so sorry I damaged it.' But then, with a flick of her hand, the fairy instantly repaired the web. 'If there is anything I can ever do for you. . . .' she added.

"Celia was astonished by the fairy's magic. Suddenly she realized how tired she was of repairing her web all the time. 'Well, there is one thing you could do,' said Celia. 'I don't mean to complain, but it seems like all I ever do is mend my web. Humans are constantly bumbling into it and tearing it to shreds. Is there anything you can do to help?'

"The tiny fairy thought a minute. 'I have an idea. What we need to do is make the web more visible to everyone but flies.' With a sweep of her hand, she transformed the web into a beaded network of dewdrops. 'Every morning your web will catch the dew, and its many strands will sparkle like jewels in the sunlight. Even when the sun hides behind the clouds, your web will delight those who are able to see it.'

"Each morning thereafter, Celia's web was a wonder to behold. The farmer noticed it every time he walked by, and the children always stopped to stare in awe at its beauty. Humans never blundered into the web again.

"This magical gift was passed on to Celia's children, and her children's children, until every web in the field was covered with morning dewdrops. If you ever see a web covered with tiny drops in the cool morning air, you too will be amazed by its beauty. You will walk around the web, respecting its wonder."

EIGHT - AND MORE - LEGGEDS IN THE MEADOW-THICKET

Some morning, when you are out walking in the early dew, look for dewdrops collecting on webs in the soft light. Do you see a pattern resembling a sunburst? Or something else? Who makes these? How many legs does the critter have? You have probably discovered that all insects have six legs, not eight. Which insect-like creatures of the meadow have more than six legs? The spider belongs to a family of animals called "invertebrates", which means they have no backbone. A walk through a meadow may reveal some of the incredible homes of these engineers.

🐚 Have you ever **observed a spider** as it weaves a web, catches food, repairs a web, or rests in ambush? Observe one in a meadow or around some outbuildings. Often a cellar provides a friendly environment for spiders. Spiders are like engineers. They skillfully design bridges, balloons, even airplanes! As you learn more about spiders, maybe you'll discover how they do this. Have you discovered where their long webs are made?

As you look into your first spider's web, take a few moments to reflect. What questions occur to you? List them in your journal before going on.

🐚 Look closely at the spider's body shape and its web. What does it remind you of? You might enjoy making a **drawing in your journal based on the symmetry** of the spider's body. Try to recreate the pattern in the web as well. Look for spirals, sunbursts, symmetrical forms.

✎ Here are some ideas for **journal writing:**

- Write about a day in the life of a spider.
  - What value do you think spiders have?
    - How does a spider

weave its web, catch its food, dispose of waste, raise its young, or survive the heavy rain?

- Did you learn the truth about any myths concerning spiders?
- How do you feel about spiders?

Carefully search for the many-leggeds besides spiders that reside in the meadow, under rocks in the yard, or in the basement or garage. **Spend some time getting to know your neighbors.** This can be a good introduction to the everyday events in the nature neighborhood that lies beneath your feet.

Math, Nature's Way

Spiders can be great subjects for creating multiplication feats. If you spied a spider egg case that had twenty baby spiders in it, how many legs would you find? Thirty? One hundred? More? Write some **spider leg math mysteries**, then try to solve them.

FOOD WEBS IN THE MEADOW - THICKET NEIGHBORHOOD!

It's amazing to discover that all living things in the meadow-thicket habitat depend upon one another for survival.

🐦 **Can you make a food web showing the relationship** between meadow plants, insects, spiders and other natural or unnatural elements found in the meadow-thicket?

To make a Food Web

You will need:

index cards
drawing materials
a ball of yarn

1) How many species of meadow-thicket neighbors can you think of? On each index card, illustrate one member of this grassy habitat.

2) When several friends are playing, each person can string yarn through an index card and wear the card as a necklace. Play in a circle on the floor. If playing alone, simply place the index cards in a circle on the floor. In both cases the object is to connect, with a ball of yarn, all of the elements that support one another in a life-giving process.

For example, a person wearing a spider index card can connect herself to the grasshopper she might eat by passing the ball of yarn to whoever is wearing a grasshopper index card. The grasshopper might then connect itself to grass by passing the yarn to the grass. The grass might connect itself to the gifts of life - sun, soil or water. Eventually a web of inter-connectedness will weave everyone together!

🐦 What do you think about this web of meadow life? What does it mean to you? How is a meadow-thicket neighborhood like a human neighborhood? How is it like a garden?

✍ You might enjoy **drawing this web of life** in your nature journal. Begin by drawing, in the center of the page, a picture of the gifts of life - sun, soil and water. What element in nature depends directly on these gifts of life? If you have chosen grass, draw some grass next to the three gifts to show that it needs them to survive. What needs grass to survive? If you have chosen grasshoppers, draw some grasshoppers in the grass. What needs grasshoppers to survive? Perhaps a garden spider! Continue drawing until your web of life grows into a "chain of inter-connectedness".

COOPERATIVE GAMES
OF THE NATURE NEIGHBORHOOD

The Iroquois Indians, or Woodlands people, often hosted cooperative athletic games and events which strengthened the individual as well as the community. Sometimes the people of a nation had to travel far as their villages were separated by great distances. But the festivities brought people together, allowing them to share ideas with like-minded individuals, as well as to enjoy the various talents displayed by the participants. Even today these events can be important community-building tools for enhancing the relationships between neighbors.

A Native American Trail Game ❧

Years ago, the Native people journeyed along footpaths to visit neighboring villages, to visit family clan members, to move from a summer to a winter camp, or to stalk past the territory of an unfriendly neighboring nation. Well-trod paths led the way, but often the people would take - for a variety of reasons - junctions, short cuts or detours.

Young Native children loved to mimic their parents through games, just as children today play dress-up and imitate adults. Native children playing along the trails probably set up trail signs, copying the ones created by the hunters and braves who set out from camp. Although these imaginary games were fun, the children were developing skills that would enable them, as adults, to read subtle trail signs.

Walking quietly and carefully enables you to develop a heightened awareness about animals that might be nearby. Learn to observe subtle animal signs, and work on your stalking skills. If you are very quiet, you might be rewarded by seeing an animal that ordinarily would be scared away by your presence!

The stalking game described below is great fun! Trail interpretation, planning, and stalking techniques influence the outcome of the game.

♠ Break up into two trail groups. While the second group covers its eyes, the first group lays out the course, using rocks or - if necessary - toothpicks as trail signs. The rocks should be set up at frequent intervals along the trail, indicating the direction of travel the second group should take. If the second group reads the trail signs correctly, the rocks will lead them to a hiding place or camp where the first group has secluded itself!

Here are some examples of rock trail signals:

This is the beginning of the trail

You are on the trail

Turn left

Danger, go back!

Turn right

♠ Before laying out a trail course, review the trail signs with the entire group so that everyone understands them. When the trail signs are set up, the first group should hide at the trail's end with their eyes closed so they cannot see the group stalking them.

♠ The second trail group stalks the first, interpreting the signs along the way. The second group must remain quiet, however, or the first trail group may stealthily relocate upon hearing them. When the first group is located, reverse roles so the second group gets a chance to set up the signs and hide.

If you substitute toothpicks or sticks for rock signs, create your own meanings. Or try these:

Three parallel sticks means: *"This is the trail"*   ▮▮▮

Crossed toothpicks means: *"Danger"*   ✕

One vertical toothpick, with another one laid horizontally to the left, means: *"Turn left"*   ▬▮

One vertical toothpick, with another one laid horizontally to the right, means: *"Turn right"*   ▮▬

A Cross-Country Challenge 🦃

Traditionally, Native villages would gather for great athletic events and to participate in cross-country challenges. Athletes would run great distances in these contests, which prepared them for the important task of running from village to village to deliver important messages.

Native children also practiced for cross-country challenges. In the evenings they would assemble with their elders, who would help them to develop athletic skills through broad jumps, high jumps, relays, obstacle races or foot races. Though lots of fun, these evening activities served as part of a physical training program in the Native community.

Then, as now, cross-country running was an incredible feat of endurance. Today, Jim Thorpe, a Native American runner, is a world renowned athlete for his record-breaking, long distance run across the United States.

(continued)

To prepare yourself for a Cross-Country Challenge, practice broad jumps, high jumps, relays and foot races!

🦌 Try this **Cross-Country Challenge**. Invite friends and neighbors - or the entire village - to a race across the land! Players can design a creative challenge course consisting of natural or human obstacles.

1) Villagers or participants divide into groups of runners, Chiefs, Clan Mothers or "obstacles".

2) Runners will compete in the cross-country challenge course.

3) Chiefs and Clan Mothers judge the events. At appropriate stations, Chiefs and Clan Mothers oversee the successful completion of an obstacle, such as a broad jump across a river, or a high jump over a stone wall. If the Chief or Clan Mother decides a runner did not successfully complete an event, the runner must try to overcome the obstacle again.

4) The "obstacles" use their bodies to create challenges for those participating in the relay course. Of course, obstacles may also consist of rope or actual landscape features.

"To the sun shall we race, before it leaves us for the moon!"

♠ Here are some suggestions for creating **cross-country obstacles:**

- **River** - two ropes, two long sticks or two bodies can delineate the width of a stream. A Chief or Clan Mother will judge a qualifying or non-qualifying leap!

- **Mountain** - a hill or a group of squatting children makes a nice mountain. Participants must "leapfrog" over the mountain.

- **Forest** - players stand closely together with "limbs" outstretched to mimic a forest. Runners must circle around the forest, or run through it along a winding path.

- **Rocky area** - chairs or hunched-over villagers can represent boulders. Participants run through the rocky area without touching the boulders. Judges must be vigilant here!

- **Anything goes** - use your imagination!

5) Clearly define the course. Explain the challenge to the entire village so that everyone understands how the course can be successfully completed.

6) At the starting gate, **runners should be staggered** so that no one leaves until the runner in front of him has entered the second obstacle area.

7) The course should be laid out so that the runners eventually circle back to the starting gate. Runners who finish the relay **greet and cheer each athlete** until all are safely home. When all the runners have completed the course, the Chiefs, the Clan Mothers and the "obstacles" run to the finish as well.

8) Traditionally, a cool drink or nourishment welcomes home all runners, judges and participants.

The game begins when the Chief or Clan Mother shouts:

"To the sun shall we race, before it leaves us for the moon!"

MORE NATURE AND
TRUST BUILDING GAMES

❧ Spider and Fly

1) Choose one member of the class to be a spider, and another a fly. The rest of the class becomes a spider web by forming a circle. The spider creeps to the center of the web and stands with its eyes closed. With the sensitivity of a critter who can feel the slightest intrusion on its web, the spider will attempt to ensnare a fly without seeing it!

2) The group making up the web should remain silent and act as a protective boundary for the blind spider. They also form the boundary within which the fly moves.

3) The fly should fly silently about the web, trying to avoid capture. If it is fortunate enough to avoid the spider for a long time, then it will grow confident and begin to buzz while flying about the web. Before long the spider should snatch the fly!

❧ The Stump

Place a two-foot wide, two-foot high wooden stump in a meadow - near an EARS station, if you wish. Can the entire group stand on the stump at the same time? No outside help is permitted. The group can use only the support of its members to accomplish this challenge. To build trust and cooperation, play the Stump challenge throughout the year.

❧ The Bear Mark

Ask anyone who has lived near bears the following question: "Where do bears spend their time?" Most likely they'll answer: "Up a tree." You can tell how high bears climb if you look for claw marks on the tree.

♠ In this game, try to reach as high as a bear can climb. First, break into two groups. With the help of an adult, or using a chair or some crates, the first group should make a mark high on a tree or on a building wall.

♠ The second group must then try to reach the mark without the help of an adult or the use of a chair or crate. Members of the group may support themselves in any way, so long as they rely only on support provided by the group. No climbing of the tree or building itself is permitted. Be creative! Take care of one another, and be sure to have spotters while climbing!

Play this game on several occasions throughout the Fall, observing how group-building techniques change and refine themselves over time. You will also be surprised to see how high the mark will go with increased, persistent efforts!

Happy Fall!

65

WINTER

"BLACK BEAR'S PLAN"

Welcome to Winter! As the days grow colder and shorter, listen as Grandforest Tree explains how the seasons came into being:

I remember my Winters as a spindly little sprout, completely covered with snow all season long. I was quite snug and warm beneath all that white fluff. The snow covered me like a blanket, protecting me from harsh winter winds. Mice, moles and squirrels benefited from the snow, too. They developed endless networks of tunnels under my safe, wintry quilt. They often visited me on the way to gather food from their caches, so I was never lonely.

"As the years passed, I grew strong enough to survive the cold. More and more of me stood above the snow, and I was able to observe the happenings across the stark, white world. . . .

"Winter is a time of stillness. The quiet strength and beauty of the landscape, free from all embellishments, reveals itself day after day. It is a time of patience and waiting, full of hope, anticipation and wonder, a time when the inner workings of Mother Nature seem to stand in frozen silence.

"But is everything really frozen and silent? As you explore Winter in the meadow-thicket, you may find that life is not so still. If you listen carefully, and if you look closely, you will discover that Winter has many stories to tell.

"Speaking of stories, I remember a tale my great-great-great-grandmother used to tell me when the snows began to fall.

"She said that a long time ago the Iroquois were excellent hunters. They hunted year-round and caught many animals. At this time, Sister Summer ruled the land for ten

months of the year, making it easy for hunters to wander wherever they wished in search of game. So ruthless were these hunters, that the animals began to fear for their survival.

"One day, Black Bear invited all the animals - even insects and birds - to her den for a meeting. 'These hunters threaten our peace and our lives,' said Black Bear. 'They pursue us relentlessly, even to our dens, so that we cannot rest or find food. I suggest we ask Sister Summer to let Brother Winter dominate the land for most of the year.'

"Black Bear's plan was fine for the larger animals, like Bear, Moose, and Coyote, whose thick fur protected them from the cold. But the smaller animals, especially those who foraged on green plants for food, objected. Rabbit spoke for them.

"'So much cold would not be good for us smaller creatures. You bigger animals have thicker fur to keep you warm, and your longer legs enable you to reach the food above the snow. And Bear, you sleep all Winter, so you do not have to worry about these things. But how will we smaller creatures obtain food if the Winters are longer and colder? And look at the little insects. How will they keep warm, with no fur at all? If we have Winter for ten months of the year, the berry bushes will not bear fruit, the grass will not grow lush and green, and the plants will not produce seeds. If there is no food for us smaller animals, we will not be able to survive - and then what will you larger animals eat?'

"The larger animals were surprised at Rabbit's wisdom. He was right - too much Winter would threaten their survival even more than the dangerous humans. They decided that Brother Winter and Sister Summer should share the wheel of the year, with six months of cold and snow so the animals could rest from being hunted, and six months of warmth so the plants could grow to feed the smaller animals. Many creatures were given gifts to stay warm during the cold months - some flew south, like the Monarch butterfly and certain species of birds. Some animals snuggled below the ground, or made tunnels beneath the snow, and some developed a thicker winter coat that blended into the desolate landscape. All the animals were satisfied. As for the humans, they were forced to spend many months of the year inside their lodges, telling stories and eating the food they had stored.

"So remember, the animals enjoy the Winter, just as you do. Watch for their stories in the snow, and keep track of what you see. I think you will be very surprised at the activity of animals during Winter."

CALENDAR OF THE NATURE NEIGHBORHOOD

The Nature Neighborhood provides seasonal wonders through-out the New Year. Make a calendar to document some of the wonders that lie ahead. If you wish, give this calendar to friends or relatives as a gift for the holidays. Groups can sell the nature calendars during the New Year as a fund raiser for a Nature Neighborhood project.

"Thirty days hath September, April, June and
November.
All the rest have thirty-one, 'cept February,
Which has twenty-eight and Leap Year twenty-nine.
If we followed the lunar rhythm,
I wouldn't have to remember this rhyme!"

A Nature Neighborhood Calendar

You will need:

twelve sheets of white, unlined
    paper
a ruler
a pencil and eraser
drawing materials
a calendar of the new year
two pieces of cardboard or
    poster board the same
    size as the calendar paper

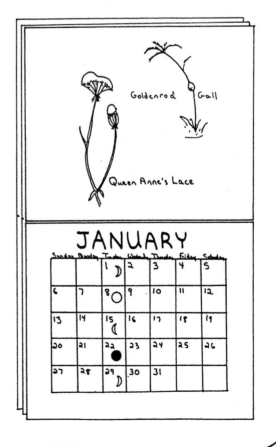

❦ On each of the twelve sheets of white, unlined paper, make seven grids for the seven days of the week, and five grids for the weeks of the month. This requires good measuring skills, so follow the directions below carefully.

1) First, measure the width of the paper to determine how many inches wide each daily box should be. (At this stage you should not be drawing lines but simply making little measurement dots with the tip of your pencil). Remember, seven boxes require eight lines, so you will need to leave a little space as a border on each side of the paper. Be certain to leave a large space at the top of the paper so you will have room to write in the name of the month and the days of the week!

2) Next, measure the length of the paper to create five sections for the five weeks of the month. Here again, make little measurement dots. Remember: five sections require six lines. Just as you did on the sides of the paper, leave a little border at the bottom of the paper.

3) The best way to draw a grid is to connect the four, outermost dots so that you have a large box. When you do this, draw the lines lightly or you will not be able to see the little measurement dots!

4) Once the box is drawn, it is time to connect the dots. Draw lines across the paper for the five weeks of the month. Then draw lines from the bottom of the paper up to make the seven days of the week. Be sure not to draw lines outside the box!

5) When the grid is finished, write the seven names of the days of the week at the top of each column.

6) Write the name of the month at the top of each calendar page, above the days of the week.

7) Now look at a calendar for the upcoming year. What day of the week does New Year's Day fall on? Write the number "1" in this box. How many days are there in January? Perhaps the rhyme will help you to remember. Continue writing the rest of the numbers of the days of January. When you've finished, you might enjoy listing interesting nature facts in the numbered boxes, such as special holidays, full moons, reminders to feed the wild birds - whatever you like!

8) What goes on in the Nature Neighborhood during the month of January? Draw something appropriate on the inside of the front poster board cover. How about dried Queen Anne's Lace poking out of the snow like a star burst? What other qualities does January possess? You can get some ideas about the qualities of all of the months by looking through the Fall activity entitled "Lunar Calendar".

(continued)

9) Continue writing the days of the months in February through December. Draw a Nature Neighborhood illustration on the back side of the previous month. For example, February's Nature Neighborhood illustration will appear on the back side of January's calendar grid. Remember to add interesting nature notes for each month.

10) The outside of the poster board covers can be illustrated as well. Write a short story about the project and the author for the inside of the cover.

11) Staple or sew together the poster board covers and the months of the year - in their proper order, of course. And Voilà! A Nature Neighborhood masterpiece made for someone special!

HOWDY, NEIGHBORS!

You can gain an awareness and appreciation for the many nearly invisible nature neighbors in the winter neighborhood simply by looking, listening, feeling and smelling!

❧ Before setting out to explore a winter neighborhood, gather together the items you will need for exploration and discovery.

You will need:

a warm, sunny winter day
warm clothing for lying down outdoors
a three-foot diameter circle of clothesline rope for each individual or each group of nature neighborhood buddies (perhaps 4 children in a group)
a hand lens
(continued)

insect magnifier boxes
journals and illustrating materials
something warm to lie upon

♠ Dividing into small groups of four creates an opportunity for cooperative learning experiences. Each group should:

- Decide how to **care for and share** the materials and tools to be used in the discovery lesson.

- Decide who will be **the recorder**, who **the timekeeper**, and who **the spokesperson** for the group that day.

- Bring along a watch, a hand lens, magnifier boxes, rope circles, journals, and any other necessary materials.

♠ Once the groups are organized, go to a nearby meadow or lawn area and explore some winter wonders. **Look for the best observation sites.** These are usually located near a bush, tree, bird feeding station, nature cafe, meadow edge, or another place where animals might like to gather. Each group should define their Nature Neighborhood area by **laying out a rope circle** in an agreed-upon location. Then all can lie stomach down around the circle, eyes closed for a minute.

- **Listen to sounds** that occur near the rope circle.

- **Sniff for odors of animals** - the scents may be only tiny amounts!

- **Now feel, with closed eyes, the sun, temperature, wind and other textures** that your nature neighbors are experiencing.

- Remember that **digging gently beneath the snow** may reveal more information.

- **Look for patterns in the snow.** What do

you think made them?

What did you discover in your Nature Neighborhood? You might see dried winter weeds or seed pods. Look for tracks of mice, chipmunks, squirrels or rabbits. You might see the runways of meadow voles. On a warm, sunny day, you might even see insects - like snow fleas or honeybees!

A Discovery Share Circle

♠ **Upon returning** from the outdoor learning sites, each group should prepare for a **Discovery Share Circle**.

1) Choose a name and logo that describes the group's Nature Neighborhood, and record the name and logo in nature journals.

2) Agree upon one special, secret nature neighbor. If possible, the nature neighbor can be brought inside and viewed with a magnifier, and its mysteries illustrated in nature journals.

3) All the cooperative learning groups should then come together in a discovery share circle, where each designated spokesperson will share the discoveries of her group.

4) One at a time, each spokesperson will introduce her group, using the name and logo which describes the group's Nature Neighborhood.

5) Next, the spokesperson will provide clues about her group's mystery neighbor, being careful not to reveal the neighbor's identity. The other cooperative learning groups will then try to guess the identity of the mystery neighbor.

6) If possible, living proof of the nature neighbor can be brought to the share circle. But don't pass around sketches or proof of the living thing until the mystery question has been answered! If no one knows the true name of the nature neighbor, make up a name that describes its qualities or characteristics.

7) At the end of the discovery lesson, everyone should record the newly-introduced nature neighbors in her journal. Try to answer the following questions about the mystery neighbor:

- What job does the neighbor perform in the neighborhood?
- Does the nature neighbor belong to a family?
- What does the nature neighbor need in order to survive the Winter?
- How am I and the nature neighbor alike?
- How well did the share circle work?

Want To Do More?

🐌 After your eyes have told you all they can, **use magnifying tools to examine** tiny insects, dried flowers, or anything else you found in the Nature Neighborhood.

- Make a list of **questions** about what you discovered.

- **Illustrate** what you saw.

- **Make rubbings** of something interesting.

- **Press a dried plant**.

- **Write poetry or a song** that comes to you.

- Enter **a story of the experience** into your journal.

✎ You might want to **record and document** your findings in your journal.

SNOOPING THROUGH THE WINTER WONDERLAND: INSECT HOUSES

Throughout Summer and Fall, the meadow was a symphony of insect calls. But in Winter their music is replaced with cold silence. Where do these many-legged critters go for a winter's rest?

🐝 It's exciting to go on a **winter insect hunt** and discover the nearly invisible world of insects.

You will need:

magnifying tools
insect boxes
drawing pads
pencils

🐝 On a warm, sunny day, when the temperatures are above freezing and everyone is bundled up for hiking, go on a nature neighbor **search for insect houses**. Bring along magnifying tools, insect boxes and, most importantly, drawing pads and pencils.

♥ If you were an insect, where would you go for a winter's

rest? Some great locations for discovering the mysteries of insects are in nearby out-buildings, or in basements or garages. Also, hike to a nearby meadow-thicket or to the forest edge. You'll be surprised at the amount of insect activity in Winter!

♥   After you have found a mysterious insect house, sit close by and quietly observe it. Look at it with eyes of wonder, searching for answers. Look at it with eyes that ask questions.

✍ Write down any questions that occur to you. If you make an illustration of the insect house mystery, it will be easier to remember the things you learn that day. When you draw the parts, capture each and every detail, as if you were the first person ever to have discovered it and may never see it again. Did you answer any of your questions in your drawing?

♥   When you are finished with the silent visitation, look one more time and ask: How am I and this mystery creature alike? Writing about the ways you resemble a winter insect may inspire a poem, a song, or a story! Record it alongside the illustration in your journal.

♥   Did you know that wonderful means "full of wonder"? What unique thing did you learn about this insect mystery that filled you with wonder? In your journal, write a story about something being "full of wonder".

When you are finished with your creative writing, tell the story in your own words.

"PETRA, THE IMPATIENT PUPA"

Grandforest Tree recounts Petra's winter dream:

The Voices of the Winds caress the air with more stories than I can possibly remember. And yet some stories traveling on the breeze are unforgettable. Here is one about Petra, an impatient Pupa who thought Spring would never arrive.

"As Winter approached, Petra, who was still a caterpillar, crawled onto a willow tree and spun a snug sleeping bag of silk. Safe in the tree, she slept soundly. The more she slept, the more her body changed. Soon she was no longer a caterpillar, but neither was she a butterfly. She was simply a pupa.

"She was very excited about becoming a butterfly, though, and could hardly wait for Spring's warm winds to beckon her from her deep slumber. She had wonderful dreams of summer meadows filled with flowers.

"As the Winter wore on, blanketing the willow tree with snow, Petra would occasionally rise from her dream world and listen for signs of Spring. But, alas, the wind howled, the snow continued to climb the willow's sturdy trunk, and the temperature plummeted.

"One January day, however, there was a thaw. The sun blazed down and the winds blew warm from the south. The birds who had remained for the Winter twittered excitedly, enjoying the break from the cold. Their singing woke Petra, who had been dreaming she floated lazily over a pond where giant water lilies bloomed. For a long moment she listened to the commotion, feeling the sun's warmth as it penetrated her soft, pupal sleeping bag.

"'Oh, my!' she thought. 'Is this it? Is it time for me to wake up?' She looked to see if she had wings, but to her disappointment she still had caterpillar feet and a cat-

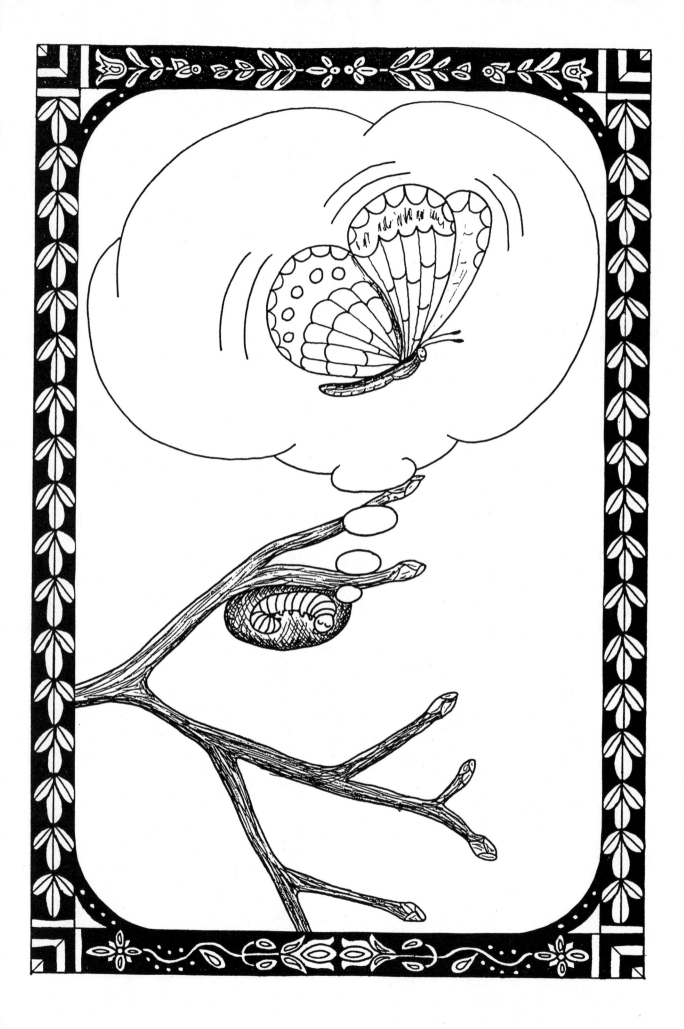

erpillar body. Her body was slowly changing shape, but it would be months before she would have a long, slender, black body and wings to fly with.

"Petra began to despair - Spring would never arrive! Or if it did, she would be more caterpillar than butterfly, and never have a chance to test her wings.

"She began to weep when a voice, penetrating her soft, silk sleeping bag, whispered to her. It was gentle Sister Spring, telling her to go back to sleep. 'Do not fear, Petra, dear. You will have wings to dance upon the winds, wings to take you to all the places you dream of. I will waken you when the time is right.'

"Sister Spring's words soothed Petra, who soon fell fast asleep, once again dreaming the Winter away.

"And indeed, just as Sister Spring promised, Petra was rewarded for her patience. That Summer she wore magnificent wings, more beautiful than any of the meadow inhabitants had ever seen. She soared and soared, happier than she had ever been in her dreams."

WINTER INSECT MYSTERIES

How do you think different kinds of insects spend the cold months?

The Meadow-Thicket hides many exciting winter insect house mysteries you can look for.

You will need:

goldenrod galls
a knife
a cutting board

In the goldenrod patch, you might notice small round bulges beneath the seed heads of dried goldenrod. These round cases are actually the Winter abode of **goldenrod gall flies**, and are called "ball galls". At Summer's end, the little larvae of the goldenrod gall fly burrow into the stem of the goldenrod plant and begin eating away. They create a neat little chamber, which, on the outside of the plant, looks like a swelling. Here the larvae snooze in a dreamy state throughout the cold Winter.

♥ To get a close up look at your nature neighbor, bring a ball gall inside. Write down your questions about this mysterious, round object. What do you think you will find inside? Cut it open, and, sure enough, in the very center you will see a curled up worm with a white head. Here the worm lives until it matures into a fly. How do you think a goldenrod gall fly gets out of its winter hotel? Look in the spring meadow for tiny holes in the gall cases, where the larvae, who become flies, once lived.

♥ Do you think galls harm the goldenrod plant? You may have noticed that many goldenrod galls lie <u>below</u> the plant's dried seeds. This means that the next generation's seeds are intact and ready, so no harm's done! After putting the goldenrod gall back together with a rubber band, you can return it to the meadow. For a special treat while you are out scouting for winter mysteries, look around for double-decker ball galls!

"Gallfly Year"

When the world was filled with birdsong
and peepers peeped,
a tiny fly flew
through
cool evening air
searching for emerging Goldenrods.

She finally found just the right one.
She laid eggs
on the growing Goldenrod stem
as a Wood Thrush warbled
at the edge of the woods.

Time passed.
At last,
on a sun-warmed morning
one tiny white worm
hatched
from an egg on the surface of the
Goldenrod stem.
The sluggish, legless little fellow
looked about
his snout sniffing the air.
He yawned, stretched,
and began to bore
through the stem's tough skin.
Inside it was warm and dry.
With a happy sigh
he curled up and slept
so soundly
he did not know
that a ball-shaped gall grew
around him.

(continued)

That Fall, when the late, lazy afternoon sun
graced the fiery Goldenrod and
the gilded-yellow centers of asters,
the tiny white worm woke and went to work.
He burrowed through the ball-shaped gall
tunneling as close as he dared to the outside
world.
Then he crept back into the center and slept,
as cold moons and snowy days passed.
Safely snuggled in his little gall-house,
he dreamed, and grew wings - wings to fly with.

When the cycle of seasons
circled to spring,
birds and peepers began to sing sweet songs.
Our tiny worm-friend began to seek
the sweet warm air.
He crawled through the tunnel he'd
made in the fall,
and began to batter the outside wall
of the gall
with a sturdy balloon at the top of his head.
After butting for hours and wondering when ?
the wall of the husk-hardy gall gave way -
AND THEN . . .
    the tiny fly flew
        through cool evening air.

J.H.

The Viceroy butterfly chrysalis is fun to find in the winter meadow. Did you know that Viceroy chrysalises emerge as butterflies and resemble the Monarch? Do you know how the Viceroy mimics the Monarch? The wing patterns are nearly identical, except the Viceroy has an additional black wing bar on its lower wing. The Viceroy also appears a lot earlier in the year than the Monarch, who migrates north from Mexico and California.

The Viceroy butterfly prefers the leaves of willow or poplar trees for its winter sleeping bag. Look around willow trees for a partial leaf, curled up tightly and wound with silky wrappings. The tiny caterpillar ate part of the leaf last Summer, then spun a silky sack and attached itself to the branch of the tree. Wrapped in a soft pupal case, the Viceroy caterpillar is now metamorphosing into the butterfly stage, and since the case is firmly attached to the branch the sleeping worm does not have to worry about falling from the tree along with the autumn leaves. Here the worm rests, waiting for Spring's signal. If you keep an eye on the pupa, in the Spring you might be lucky enough to see a mature butterfly emerge from its sleeping bag!

Snow fleas are some of the tiniest and fastest insects you'll see in the Winter, not to mention one of the few moving insects this time of year! You'll have to think small to notice them because they look like grains of pepper bouncing around on a snowbank. Fortunately, they like to hang out in large groups, otherwise you might never see them at all. If you think you've found some, move your hand along the snow where the pepper seems to be. If the jumping, pepper-like spots are there one minute but not the next, you can be pretty sure you've found Snow fleas! Allow a group of Snow fleas to land on your hand. They won't bite you, but they do like to feed on decaying vegetation. If you're lucky enough to catch one in an insect magnifying box, observe their springtail motion. This is how they get around!

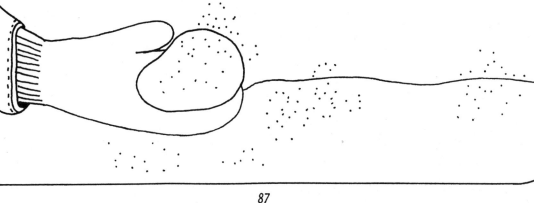

√ **Praying mantis** cases are quite interesting. You might find one on a twig in the meadow. If you notice a cocoon that is tan in color, and seems to have a foam-like case with ripples running through it, you have found the winter resting place for praying mantis eggs! Many eggs are laid in the case, which has a channel running through its center. This is the escape route for emerging baby mantises. When is a good time for them to emerge? Did you know that in many states praying mantises are a protected species? Do some research about the wonderful assistance mantises provide to farmers and gardeners.

√ **Spider egg cases** that belong to the brilliant, yellow and black Garden Spider can be found in the winter meadow-thicket. Remember, spiders are not insects. The egg cases of these hardy, mysterious neighbors are not hard to see, for they are nearly the size of a pingpong ball. The tan egg sacks are attached to grasses with strong silk. Did you know that the spiders are alive and well inside, and that the strongest spiders eat the weak? The egg sacks are full of activity! You can guess what happens in the Spring! Once again their beautiful, circular webs - which consist of zigzag, ladder-shaped designs spreading out from the center - will be seen in the meadow-thicket.

√ **Honeybees** take advantage of the first warm, sunny day to fly from the cramped quarters of their winter nest. Of course, only the Queen and the worker bees live through the Winter, surviving on the stored honey in their nests. The drones were kicked out in the Autumn because otherwise they would consume too much honey. Did you ever wonder where bees go in Winter and what they do? Observe their travels and you will learn something!

♥ To attract honeybees to a place where you can readily observe them, place a dish of honey outdoors. Now be patient and wait for the first bee. Where does it go when it leaves the dish? How long before the next bee arrives? How did the second bee know where to find the dish?

Bees communicate the whereabouts of fields of flowers to other bees of their colony. **Observe their behavior** for clues about bee communication. Do you see the bees doing a dance in flight? How might you describe it? If the honey source is close by, they do a circular dance. If the honey source is far away, they perform a figure eight dance. This is a simple description of the communication method bees use to describe the location of nectar. But bees make other, finer movements. By suddenly changing direction to create angles of flight, bees practically map out directions in mid-air! Amazing or not?

A Bee Dance

Try the following activity. Choreograph a dance that will signal flower locations to your fellow bees. Can you develop a communication dance to explain exactly how to find the honey source?

1) First, decide on the location of the hive, the honey source, and other landmarks, such as a tree.
- How would you communicate the directions?
- What signals could you use for left? Right? How would you indicate a tree, a stone wall or other features?
- How would you communicate: "Go directly ahead to the tree"?
- How would you signal: "Turn left toward the meadow"?

2) Now put all of your signals together so you can do a bee dance buzzing from your hive, around trees and over fences until you arrive at a sweet honey spot. Don't forget to turn around and take that honey home again!

🐝 Where are the winter insects that you don't see? What insect mysteries do you find amazing? Could you live in a world without insects? Do you think your size has any relationship to the value you add to the world?

Math, Nature's Way.

🐝 Look at pictures of Snow fleas, Viceroy butterflies, honeybees, and Garden spiders. Do they look **symmetrical**? In other words, is one half of their body identical to the other half? Place a drawing of one of these insects on a table, then hold a mirror vertically along the middle of the insect's back. Now do you understand what symmetry means?

✍ Enter symmetrical drawings of each of these insects in your journals. First, draw one half of the body, then copy the other half.

🐝 Record in **nature journals** the life cycles of insects discovered in the meadow-thicket. Insects have either a complete or an incomplete cycle of metamorphosis. Illustrate an example of a **complete metamorphosis**. For example, a butterfly or a honeybee passes through the stages of egg - larva - pupa - adult, which constitutes a complete metamorphosis cycle. Now illustrate an **incomplete metamorphosis**. Grasshoppers exhibit an incomplete metamorphosis cycle as they pass through the stages of egg - young adult - adult.

CARETAKING WINTER WONDERS:
A WINTER TERRARIUM

If the weather prevents you from making regular visits to the meadow-thicket, make a small terrarium and place your outdoor findings in it. A terrarium will enable you to observe egg cases as they pass through the seasonal rhythms that form an insect's life cycle.

🐛 When you take a creature from its place in nature, you become responsible for its well-being. A helpful question to ask yourself is: Do I know enough about caring for this creature to insure its prolonged life, just as Mother Nature does?

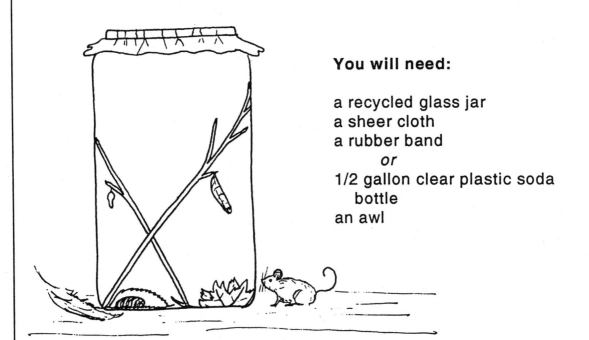

You will need:

a recycled glass jar
a sheer cloth
a rubber band
　　　　or
1/2 gallon clear plastic soda
　　bottle
an awl

1) A recycled glass jar or half gallon plastic soda bottle makes a good terrarium. Be sure the terrarium has plenty of ventilation. If you are using a glass jar, cover it with a sheer cloth and secure the cloth with a rubber band. If you are using a plastic soda bottle, poke holes in it with an awl.

2) Keep the terrarium outside and out of direct sunlight to insure that it does not overheat. Protect the terrarium so that it does not fill up with rain or snow, which might freeze and crack it. Visit your winter guest daily. Care for its needs. Record any observations in your nature journal. By returning your six-legged friends to their original habitat when you are finished, you will insure that they will be close to their food source and other necessities.

    Long ago, Native American children didn't make terrariums. How did children and adults pass the long, cold Winter back then? **Storytellers** would warm the hearts of those sitting around the winter fire, entertaining them from the first frost to the last with magical stories of insects and animals. Can you tell some of your favorite stories about insects, animals or other winter mysteries?

    Native people also passed the Winter by playing simple games made with gifts from the Earth. These games and toys were believed to be special gifts given to the people by certain nature spirits. For example, Native peoples believed that the Spider People passed down the string game known as Cat's Cradle. Play Cat's Cradle - and amazing web-shaped images will appear before your eyes! You'll need a spider partner to help you weave fascinating Cat's Cradle webs.

For Cat's Cradle fun, read Cat's Cradles, Owl's Eyes: A Book of String Games, *by Camilla Gryski.*

92

NATURE CAFÉS:
WILDLIFE FEEDERS

If you would like to see some hidden winter animals and have a chance to care for them, create a Nature Café that attracts country - and even urban - wildlife!

February is often known as the Hunger Moon among Native peoples. What do you think this means? To discover and support some of Winter's hungry, active animals, you can design several wildlife feeders for the Nature Café. This activity can be done alone or with a group of friends. Imagine beforehand the type of animal you would like to attract. This will help you determine the appropriate height and function of each feeder.

🐦 Try the following suggestions to make an animal feeder - or create your own!

Animal Feeders

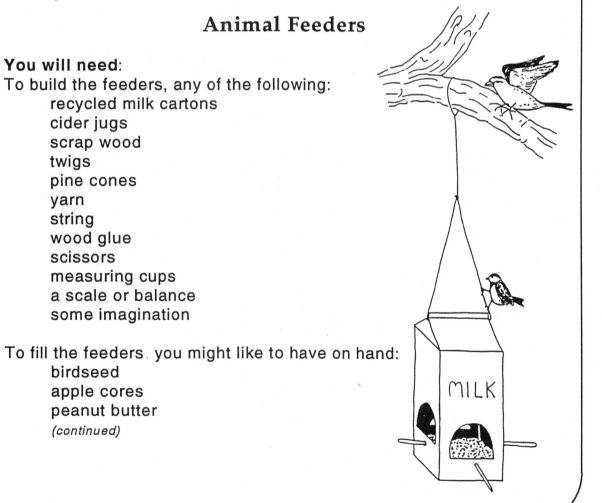

You will need:
To build the feeders, any of the following:
     recycled milk cartons
     cider jugs
     scrap wood
     twigs
     pine cones
     yarn
     string
     wood glue
     scissors
     measuring cups
     a scale or balance
     some imagination

To fill the feeders, you might like to have on hand:
     birdseed
     apple cores
     peanut butter
(continued)

popcorn and cranberries
dried ears of corn
shelled nuts
citrus hulls

To make maps and record findings:
large paper
colored pencils

> ☞ *You can design all kinds of feeders, but please avoid using metal as tiny paws and tongues may adhere to these frosty surfaces!*

🐦 When determining **a location for the Nature Café**, choose a tucked away spot that will provide protection or privacy for the animals, but be sure it is within visiting distance. A screen of trees or bushes will enable you to see what's going on without disturbing your friends. Hang up your feeders and watch your hidden winter nature neighbors come for a bite to eat. Make a Nature Café sign and post it at the Nature Neighborhood. *Now the adventure begins!*

♥ Dried ears of corn may be hung from trees to attract raccoons and woodpeckers. Hang some ears low enough for a raccoon to reach. Suspend some old bagels from a tree, too.

♥ Place lunch scraps nearby on the ground.

♥ Chipmunks love shelled nuts, so scatter some on the ground.

♥ Old apples and apple cores attract deer. Place these in open, meadow-like places.

♥ Make birdseed feeders from milk cartons and cider jugs.

♥ From trees, hang citrus hulls filled with peanut butter, seeds, stale nuts, or cranberries. Smear pine cones with peanut butter and bird seed, and hang them on a nearby tree. String popcorn and cranberries between two trees.

❧ **Daily observations** will show what's been eaten from the café as well as who might have visited. Look for any tracks or scat nearby. What you discover may be hard to believe, so you may want to document your findings. To record your observations, you might want to:

♥   Make a map of the wildlife feeding area. Record tracks and mark them on your map.

❧ Can you answer the following **mystery questions** about your Nature Neighborhood?

- Who visits the Nature Neighborhood?
- What do nature neighbors eat?
- What kinds of families live in the Nature Neighborhood?
- How do these nature neighbors adapt to the winter weather?

Math, Nature's Way

❧   Measure and weigh the amount of food eaten each day. Keep a record of this for a month or more. Graph the results based on weekly consumptions. Is there a pattern to how much food is eaten? Does it seem like the birds are eating more as the Winter progresses? Or less? Why do you think this is so?

♥   Draw up a menu of the foods offered at the Nature cafes. Record any changes, as well as the frequency of feedings. The types and amount of food eaten can be portrayed by making a bar graph.

❧ *The many exciting things you discover in your Nature Neighborhood will demonstrate that winter wildlife is not quiet at all, simply hidden from view. Don't forget to keep the café well stocked with food, or your nature neighbors may decide to dine elsewhere!*

WILDLIFE PIZZA PUZZLES

Every animal's diet is especially suited to its needs. The amount of fat, protein and sugar differs for each animal. What have you discovered about the different diets of the meadow animals that have been attracted to your Nature Café?

🐒 What seems to be the favorite food of the animals who visit the Nature Café? Can you create wildlife pizza puzzles that represent the ingredients of each animal's diet? Once you have made these pizza-like puzzles, take them apart. Then mix up the pieces and try to figure out who eats what.

You will need:

Red cardboard
White cardboard
Nature magazine photos

Here's how to make a Wildlife Pizza Puzzle:

1) To create the pizza, cut red cardboard into a circular shape. Use white cardboard to make the edges of the pizza crust.

2) Look through nature magazines for pictures of wild animals who live in your region. Cut out pictures of food ingredients that these animals like to eat.

3) Glue the picture of one animal onto the back of a pizza. Choose pictures or drawings of foods that that particular animal likes to eat. Glue the food onto the front of the pizza (one picture or drawing for each slice!). When the glue is dry, slice the pizza.

4) Now create another pizza for another animal. Make several more pizzas, representing different animals and the foods they like best.

5) When all the pizzas are complete, mix up the pieces of the different wildlife pizzas. Then try to put them together according to each animal's favored diet. If you guess correctly, the picture of the animal appearing on the reverse side will be complete.

For example: One of the first strong scents of late Winter is the aroma of a skunk. What ingredients might be included in **a Skunk Pizza?** Fruit (from the compost pile, garbage heap or nearby bush), insect larvae, frogs, toads and mice make up this recipe. Using a large piece of red cardboard, cut out a circular pizza shape and attach the white crust border. On the back of the pizza, paste a magazine photo of a skunk. On the front side, glue magazine pictures of the food skunks like to eat. Slice when completely dry.

🐾 **Raccoon Pizza** is very flavorful. Raccoons forage around the compost heap all Winter. But if Mother Nature had to provide all the ingredients raccoons like to eat, their diet would include apples, fruits of trees and shrubs, various plants, insect grubs, fish, amphibians, even a wood duck! Make the same size and color pizza as you did for the skunk pizza, but this time add the ingredients a raccoon might eat, and paste its picture on the back.

🐾 **Chipmunk Chewy Choice Pizza** might include morsels of fruits and nuts of local trees, insects and seeds. To make the chipmunk pizza, follow the directions as above.

🐾 **Delectable Delicious Deer Pizza** includes this season's fresh and tasty Staghorn fruits, branches of bushes, grasses, lichen, and savory herbs. Don't forget to offer a refreshing drink of clear, sparkling water to wash down this rather dry recipe. Make another pizza puzzle as before.

(continued)

🐦 Do you think an animal's diet is the same year-round? Which foods in an animal's diet are found year-round? Which foods make up a winter diet?

🐦 How about your diet in Winter? Do you eat differently in Winter than in other seasons? Where does your food come from in Winter? Do you eat more fats, protein, and sugars?

NATURE NEIGHBORHOOD MANDALA

Have you ever seen so many different kinds of plants and animals and insects all living together? Have you ever stopped to think about the relationship they all have with one another?

Now that you've had a chance to observe some of the nature neighbors visiting your cafe, create a Web of Life mandala to demonstrate the interconnectedness of these animals.

But before beginning work, **listen to Grandforest Tree's story** about the web of life in the meadow-thicket. Then you can create a mandala that tells the story in pictures.

M any, many Winters have passed since I first grew tall enough to see what was happening above the snow. Being still and quiet and watchful, I have seen much. This is a story about something that actually happened a year or two ago, deep in the heart of Winter.

"All Fall the mice gathered seeds which had been dropped by the grasses. As Winter approached, some of the grasses still poked their heads above the snow as a reminder of the Summer's bounty, so the mice continued to frolic, eating and gathering seeds.

"One warm, moonlit winter evening the wee ones were out and about, scampering over the snow, leaving their tracks wherever they went. The rabbits bounded around as well, munching on twigs and the bark of the youngest trees. Everyone seemed calm and happy to be out in the night air.

"Suddenly, I spied Fox lurking near the old stone wall. She watched the moonlit antics of the small animals, licking her chops in anticipation of a meal. Slowly, slowly, she sneaked toward the oblivious mice and ignorant rabbits until, with a flying leap, she pounced on the nearest rabbit, who screamed in surprise and terror. The screams died away as Fox carried the freshly-killed meat to her den.

"The meadow was quiet for a while after that. The moon, so bright that the snow sparkled like diamonds, slid across the night sky. I heard some coyotes in the forest, not far away. Then, just when I thought the activity was over for the night, a deer sauntered into the field searching for fallen apples. I was concerned, because deer tend to travel in herds in Winter, and rarely leave the protection of the forest. Moreover, I knew the coyotes were close by.

"Sure enough, before long several coyotes appeared at the edge of the meadow-thicket - perhaps Fox had tipped them off about the abundance of small animals playing in the moonlight.

"The deer perked up her ears and tensed her body as she caught the scent of danger. Snorting, she began to run, but the coyotes quickly surrounded and trapped her. They brought her down and killed her instantly, then sat in the snow for a mid-winter meal.

"It was almost dawn by the time they had had their fill. Gray light crept in from the east, and soon the sun climbed above the ridge to cast blue shadows upon the snow. Several scavenging ravens and crows gathered to finish off what the coyotes had left.

"That afternoon the field was quiet again, but the snow told stories of all that had happened, for many of the animals had left droppings as well as tracks. But unlike the tracks, which disappeared after the next snowfall, the droppings remained. When Spring arrived and the snow melted, the droppings were absorbed by the earth, nourishing the soil where the grasses and plants grew.

"I was sorry to see my gentle friends, the rabbit and the deer, killed by the fox and the coyotes. Yet I know their deaths helped others to live. And so life goes, round and round in a great mandala."

A Web of Life Mandala

You will need:

nature journals
colored pencils or crayons

🐦 The following instructions can be used as a guide for drawing a representation of a Web of Life mandala in your nature journal. The drawing will demonstrate the interdependence of life in the Nature Neighborhood.

1) At the center of a page, draw a picture of the sun. Around the sun, illustrate leaves piled beneath the snow.

2) Next, draw snow-encrusted grasses dropping their seeds for Mouse to eat. You can show her gathering these seeds. Or draw some pictures of the corn you left out for her.

3) Illustrate Rabbit chewing the bark and twigs of bare-branched, winter trees. Don't forget to include Fox wandering through the circle looking for Mouse! Who else might come to dine on the tree's offerings? Sometimes Deer browse on fallen apples.

4) What might prey on fleet-footed Deer? You might draw Coyote lurking about, looking for a meal of deer meat. The remains of Deer's body might be scavenged by Raven and Crow. Raven and Crow's droppings nourish the soil that the grass grows in. What do you think will happen next? The circle goes round and round in the great mandala Web of Life.

"THE STORY OF JUMPING MOUSE"

Grandforest Tree has seen far and wide, but one day he watched a little tiny mouse learn to see just as far and wide.

I may be an old tree, and I may be a great tree, but nothing gives me more pleasure than to look way, way down to see my friend Little Mouse, hopping about my toes. What an engaging little creature he is! Which reminds me of a story. . . .

"Once there was a little mouse with soft brown fur, a white belly, black beady eyes and a long skinny tail. His name was Little Mouse and he was always busy, sniffing this, investigating that, looking for food, collecting seeds for winter, or adding bits of cattail fluff to warm his nest. He could be seen here and there and every where, climbing trees, scampering over logs, scurrying across the field, hurrying for reasons only he knew.

"Little Mouse was constantly in motion. Every once in a while, however, he would stop and perk up his ears, little nose twitching as he sniffed the air. As time passed he would hesitate, in this curious way, more and more often. The other animals began to notice.

"One day, Sassy Jay flew down beside him and squawked so everyone could hear. 'Little Mouse, you fool, what <u>are</u> you doing?'

"'Oh,' said Little Mouse, 'I am listening. I hear a roaring, and I am curious about what it could be.

"'That,' said Sassy Jay, 'Is the Great River. But mice don't have any business with rivers. Stop your silly listening and get on with mouse business.'

"Well, this of course made Little Mouse even <u>more</u> curious. He went to Raccoon and asked, 'Raccoon what is

a river? Sassy Jay tells me that the roaring I hear is a river.'

"Raccoon replied in a kind voice, for he was much friendlier than Sassy Jay and was quite fond of Little Mouse. 'Well, little brother, a river is something that is best seen rather than explained. Come with me and I shall show you.'

"So Little Mouse followed Raccoon down the path to the River. It was a long way and Little Mouse smelled many strange smells and saw many curious things. All of which he wanted to investigate, of course. But he was following Raccoon who ambled along at a pace that did not allow for stopping. And despite his curiosity, Little Mouse was a little fearful of all these new things.

"The mysterious roaring became much louder as they neared the river. Finally they arrived! Little Mouse shook with excitement. He followed Raccoon up a grizzly old tree to have a better look. Below them, the river frothed and heaved. Beyond, the river flowed slowly and smoothly, reflecting the sky. Little Mouse gasped with awe. 'Oh, it - it is magnificent! And powerful!!'

"'Yes, it is a wondrous thing. Come, meet my friend Frog.' Raccoon clambered down the aging tree and Little Mouse followed him to the quiet part of the river. There sat Frog on a lily-pad drying off from a swim. He greeted Little Mouse with a broad, warm smile. 'Greetings, Little Brother! Welcome to the river!

"Little Mouse returned his greeting shyly, for he was still a little fearful of the great flowing water, even though it was shallower here. He wandered over to Raccoon, who was taking a long drink, his little pink tongue lapping the water.

"Little Mouse looked down into the water and was startled to see another surprised little Mouse. 'Oh, excuse me!', said Little Mouse to his own reflection.

"'Do not be afraid, Little Mouse,' said Frog. 'That is you, reflected in the river-mirror. Don't you see Raccoon in the water, too?'

"Little Mouse cautiously moved back to the water's edge. There he saw the mouse-face again, and next to it, a raccoon washing its hands - just what Raccoon was doing at that very moment. 'Oh,' said Litlte Mouse, feeling a little silly. Glancing at Frog, who seemed to be a long way from shore, he asked, 'Aren't you frightened about being so far out in the river?'

"'Why, no,' replied Frog. 'In fact, I like it out here! You were given gifts that enable you to scamper over logs and run through the meadow, safely hidden in the grasses. I was given other gifts. This shiny-green body of mine was made for getting wet - I can live both above and below the water, swim and hop about. I could never live out of the water for long, just as you could never live in the water for very long.'

"Frog paused to consider his little mouse-friend. 'Would you like another gift?'

"'Oh, yes!' replied Little Mouse, hoping perhaps Frog's gift would make him less fearful of the river.

"'Crouch down low, and then jump up as high as you possibly can.'

"Little Mouse did so, and when he reached the apex of his jump he saw. . . . the Sacred Mountains! Oh, what a wonderful sight! However, his excitement ended rather abruptly when he landed in the water. Terrified, he scrambled from the water onto dry land. 'You, you tricked me!' screamed a very angry Little Mouse.

"Frog let Little Mouse vent his anger for a minute before he said anything. 'Hey, little Brother, you are not harmed, are you? Do not let fear and anger blind you. What did you see?'

"Little Mouse calmed down immediately. 'I - I saw the Sacred Mountains!'

"It dawned on him how his fear had been greater than the gift of seeing the dazzling snow-covered giants.

"'And now you have a new name - Jumping Mouse!

I know you will wear your name honorably,' congratulated Frog.

"'Oh, why thank you!' responded Jumping Mouse with pleasure. 'I would like to. . . . do you think I could. . .well, return to my people and tell them what I have seen?'

"'Of course!' replied Frog. 'Have a safe journey home now.' Raccoon had wandered off some time ago in search of things to eat along the riverbank. 'Remember, keep the music of the river behind you, and you will find your way home.'

"Filled with excitement, Jumping Mouse quickly returned home. But when he told his mice brothers and sisters about his adventures, no one would believe him! Saddened, Jumping Mouse returned to his den where, exhausted from his journey, he feel into a deep sleep.

"Jumping Mouse never forgot his vision of the Sacred Mountains. Indeed, every once in awhile he would jump high in the air, hoping to catch a glimpse of them.

"And so he continues this practice to this day. In fact, if you see Jumping Mouse, you might be lucky enough to catch him leaping high, trying to glimpse the Sacred Mountains!"

WHOSE TRACK IS THAT?

There are days in the Winter when the outdoors seems truly lifeless. Have you ever tried to observe signs of winter life in the forest or in the meadow-thicket? Where do the inhabitants go? How do animals survive? Think up a list of ideas about what happens to forest and meadow-thicket animals in Winter.

Some animals hibernate. Most mammals, though, are still partially active. What does a hibernating animal do in Winter? What are the activities of animals who do not hibernate? Let's take a look at Woodchuck, Jumping Mouse, House Mouse, Dormouse, Harvest Mouse, Gray Squirrel, Vole, Red Fox, and White-tailed Deer to see how they survive the Winter.

Woodchuck ❧

In the Northeast, **Woodchuck** hibernates until late February or early March. How is it, then, that Woodchuck supposedly comes out on Ground Hog's Day and looks for a shadow that tells it to go back to sleep for six weeks?

♥ **What is happening to Woodchuck during hibernation?** Well, the beating of its heart is so faint it can barely be detected. In this deep state of inactivity, there is little need for nourishment. Woodchuck seems barely alive.

♥ **What keeps him alive?** Is it the fat stored in Woodchuck's body? All Summer and Fall, before retiring to his den in October, Woodchuck feasted on meadow grasses and clover - maybe even some garden delights. Do you think it coincidental that the hibernating season begins as the garden season ends? While hibernating, fattened Woodchuck rests in its den, safe from Fox and disgruntled gardener!

♥ **Have you ever come across Woodchuck's den in the meadow?** Often you will see it near a fence or a pile of stones. When Woodchuck digs its burrow, it leaves a heap of excavated soil near the entrance. Not far from the entrance the tunnel begins to rise, which ensures that flooding waters will not fill the den. Above the water line is a nest for a pair of adults, and perhaps another nest for their young. Each nest is made from soft grasses gathered from the meadow. Woodchuck's burrow has more than one emergency exit. It's fun to try to locate these exits, for they are not nearly as visible as the front door.

When Woodchuck rises in late Winter, whether he sees his shadow or not, he doesn't have time for a six-week snooze - no matter what the weather forecaster says! March to May is the busy season for birthing young Woodchucks, and then it's on to the lush meadow and garden greens of Summer!

✍ **Can you draw Woodchuck hibernating in his burrow?** It might be fun to write about how Woodchuck's body survives during hibernation. Draw Woodchuck dreaming about the adventures he'll have when his hibernation is over.

Jumping Mouse 🐾

Jumping Mouse is often seen scurrying through the meadow or the forest. Actually, Jumping Mouse is a kangaroo mouse. If you see him, you'll understand how he got his name. Look for a tiny, three-inch long mouse whose tail is longer than his body. This wonderfully long tail, a genetic adaptation, makes him a great leaper. In fact, Jumping Mouse can jump ten feet in a single leap! With tiny front legs and strong, large rear legs, he almost looks like a miniature kangaroo. He has yellow-brown fur on his back, and yellow-golden fur on his belly. Jumping Mouse has many cousins. There are both meadow and woodland Jumping Mice. There is also a desert kangaroo mouse, whose relative, the gerbil, we keep as a house pet.

♥ **What does Jumping Mouse do all year round?** All Summer and Fall, tiny Jumping Mouse spends his days eating seeds, insects and flowers so he can fatten up by Autumn's end. What happens to Jumping Mouse during Winter? Once he reaches a certain level of plumpness, Jumping Mouse hibernates in a burrow beneath the ground. After closing the tunnel opening to protect himself from invaders, Jumping Mouse sleeps on a warm nest of grasses below the entrance. Here he lies curled into a tight, plump ball, getting thinner and thinner. When the fat stored in his body is used up, Spring calls him from his sleep. The mating season is in early Spring. If you enjoy evening walks beneath the full moon, you might be lucky enough to observe the moonlight dances of Jumping Mouse as he leaps about casting shadows in the meadow.

♥ **To learn firsthand about the fascinating world of Jumping Mouse,** it might be fun to keep a pair of **gerbils**. Observe their nest building behaviors, tunnel dwellings, and food stash habits. To supplement their bedding, offer the gerbils cardboard tubes from toilet paper rolls, cotton scraps and straw. Watch what they do with these materials as they attempt to recreate their natural environment inside the cage. Of course, you will not be able to observe any hibernating behaviors, but their behavior during other seasons is more fun to watch!

House Mouse 🐾

Other mice remain active all Winter. Even in the city you can see **House Mouse** tracks around buildings. Mouse means "thief" in Sanskrit, and this describes some aspects of House Mouse. But House Mouse is also an acrobat, and a fine friend to observe during her comings and goings.

♥ **Where does House Mouse live?** House Mouse is an incredible survivor. Long ago, when the Earth was less devel-

oped and much of the land remained wild, House Mouse popu-
lated the countrysides and forests. When humans starting
clearing the forests and meadows for dwellings, much of
House Mouse's territory was destroyed. Luckily for House
Mouse, human dwellings are fine accommodations for raising a
family. So House Mouse moved into houses, barns, ware-
houses, shipyards and the like.

♥ **How can House Mouse live in so many different places?**
Several adaptations enabled House Mouse to make this
change from one habitat to another. House Mouse eats anything - seeds, cookies, candles, paper, old socks. And all she
needs for raising a family is a sheltered spot, like your kitchen
cupboard. Being an excellent climber, she can get about
without any assistance from you. Her tail helps her to climb in
several ways. First - and you've probably never seen this
unless you lie awake in the kitchen at night waiting for House
Mouse acrobat shows - House Mouse can wrap her tail around
objects to lower or lift herself. She does this by gripping objects with her tail scales. To go forward, she simply lays her
scales smooth. To go backwards, she ruffles the scales to
improve her grip. And since she is nocturnal, she has little to
fear. Except for the occasional house cat hunting in the moonlight, she pretty much has free run of the house.

Dormouse 🐾

You might wonder: Where are all the wild mice who do not hibernate during Winter? For example, take **Dormouse**, which is French for "sleeping mouse". Dormouse is a tree dweller who looks like a squirrel, fluffy tail and all, except he is the size of a typical mouse. Like squirrels, Dormouse feasts on nuts, seeds, and fruits until the cold season arrives. Once fattened up from an abundant Summer and Fall, he wraps his furry tail around him and sleeps in a tree nest most of the Winter. If he awakens, he simply nibbles on his stash of food and goes back to sleep until Spring. Look for tree nests of Dormouse during winter forest hikes.

Harvest Mouse 🐾

One mouse you might be able to observe after Winter's end is **Harvest Mouse**. Harvest Mouse is the grass acrobat who builds her nests in the tall meadow grasses. You might see a woven grass nest in the shape of a ball swinging like a hammock between some growing grasses. Herein lie the finely shredded grasses and leaves that cradle the young nursing mice and their mother. Please do not disturb!

🐾 *Native people hold the animal nation in high regard, as animals* are viewed as relatives in the family of life. Each animal is respected for its wisdom, and the teachings of animals often serve as healing medicine for the human community. What, you might ask, can be learned from a mouse? Consider what you've learned from your observations of meadow mice or gerbils. Does Mouse live in a world where the tiniest details loom before his nose? Mouse has an ability to notice things that might go unnoticed by humans, but which have great meaning for him. Do the everyday details of your life become something you take for granted after a while? Do you sometimes scurry and hurry through your life, like a busy mouse, but without his ability to stop and notice the life around him? Do you sometimes forget to appreciate the wonder of it all?

Gray Squirrel 🐾

Gray Squirrel's homeland is often the city green or backyard, though she also enjoys the forest. Not even Winter can hide Squirrel from your view. Although often snug in a leafy nest in a tree top, Squirrel comes out sniffing for the nuts she stashed away during Autumn. On a hike one day, look for a tiny hole dug into the Earth. This is the spot where long ago Squirrel dug and buried a lone nut, but recently unearthed it for a winter feast. On a sunny day you might see Squirrel sitting in a bare tree with its bushy tail wrapped like a scarf around her neck. There's nothing like Nature's adaptations for keeping warm in Winter. Look for Squirrel's tracks. They are easy to identify as they usually begin and end between two trees!

Meadow Vole 🐭

One common, active meadow mammal is the **Meadow Vole**. Vole leaves a curious trail across the meadow, one that provides great enjoyment for the winter wildlife detective! Have you ever seen runways underneath but near the surface of the snow, zigzagging everywhere? Follow Vole's elaborate runway system and see what you can find out.

♥ **What are these runways for?** This system of zigzagging runways beneath the snow allows the six-inch long, chestnut brown or gray Meadow Vole to move about undetected by his predators. In the warm insulation of the snow runway, Meadow Vole builds a nest woven of grasses and rootlets. This ball of grass, hollowed out inside, is lined with soft grassy fibers, which creates a perfect winter sleeping bag for the tiny creature. Look around the runways for a bulging, ball-like shape. Is there a nest underneath? Search along the runways for a cache - that is, a winter food storage area. What types of food do you see in this winter pantry? What goes in must come out, so look for Vole's tiny droppings at the crossroads of the runways! Though a little sleepy at times, this animal is active in Winter.

✎ **Can you draw a map of Vole's runways in your nature journal?** Include a drawing of the tiny Meadow Vole, its nest, food and droppings.

Red Fox 🐾

Red Fox is an animal that is often seen during the winter days. This playful, curious and hungry mammal comes out of her den regularly in search of rabbits, mice, meadow voles, birds and - occasionally - a chicken. Red Fox must do a lot of stalking, as generally her prey is safely hidden in underground burrows during Winter. But chickens may be an easier find for hungry Red Fox. Although many a farmer despises Fox, the farmer should not forget how many mice Fox eats! Sometimes Fox stores food by piling it and then covering it lightly with some earth. Later, on a poor hunting day, Fox will return to this hidden cache. If she is lucky, Fox might find other animals helping themselves to the cache. For the quick Fox, this could mean a fresh meal after all!

♥ **Can you find Red Fox's tracks?** Look for Red Fox tracks in the fresh snow. Her tracks are usually patterned in a line, one paw print in front of the other. If you are lucky enough to track Red Fox back to her home, you might find that the den is in an open field or hillside. If you think the den looks like a woodchuck's burrow, you might be right! Sometimes Red Fox uses an old woodchuck burrow for her winter home, lining it with grasses.

♥ **How does Red Fox keep warm during the bitter, cold Winter?** One of her genetic adaptations - her beautiful, bushy tail - provides warmth as Fox wraps it about herself during sleep. The dark-tipped fur found on her ear and tail attracts the sun and hold its warmth, preventing frostbite.

Wear light-colored clothing in cold-yet-sunny Winter weather. Now wear dark clothing. Does one color makes you warmer than another? Can you capture some of Red Fox's beauty and natural protection in a drawing in your journal?

♥ **Do you know what Red Fox's scat looks like?** While out on Red Fox's trail, look for scat, or fox droppings. They are about four inches long and tapered at the ends, often containing berry seeds and fruit skins, as well as fur.

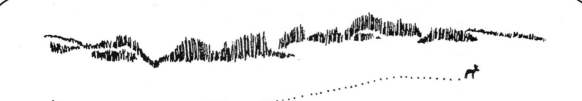

White Tailed Deer 🐾

White Tailed Deer tracks are often seen in the crisp snow. Deer wander through the meadow, but they spend most of their days in the protection of the forest. They also spend a good part of the Winter with other deer, in herds, feeding in deer yards. A deer yard is an area, usually enclosed by evergreens, where the deer are sheltered from heavy snows and bitter winds. What do you think deer eat during Winter? Deer do not paw through the deep snow to get at the grasses. They forage on tender twigs in the deer yard, sometimes depleting the entire food supply in the yard before the season ends. What happens to the deer then?

♥ **Can deer find food to eat in the meadow-thicket?** In Winter, some deer will venture into a barely protected meadow area or into old apple orchards in search of food. How does their winter coat protect them from detection in the open meadow? Their gray coat consists of coarse hollow hair. This coat not only insulates them well from the bitter cold, it helps camouflage them so they blend with the dullness of the winter meadow-thicket.

♥ **What do deer hoof prints look like?** These narrow, symmetrical tracks are two- to three-inch long, oval-shaped hoof marks with sharp points at the top.

♥ **Do you see any droppings in the snow?** Deer droppings, often found in clusters, are small oval-shaped, inch-long pellets.

♥ **Do you see any signs of deer browsing?** Tips of branches of trees and shrubs are often nibbled upon by hungry deer searching for buds and fruits. Look for these signs on Apple trees, Staghorn Sumac, and Cedar. Draw these deer foods in your journal.

✍ **Illustrate deer foraging for food during the Winter.** Draw their camouflage colors blending with the winter meadow-thicket.

(continued)

Want To Do More?

To find out more about the teachings from mice or other meadow animals, read animal fables. Or read Native American legends about animals, especially _Jumping Mouse_, a wonderful story of mouse adventures in the Great Plains - the great grasslands of the United States. See the bibliography for references.

NATURE GAMES IN WINTER

If you look carefully at the tracks of the mice, rabbits, and other creatures of the Meadow-Thicket, it might seem as though they were playing games! Take a hint from these meadow creatures, and come on outside for some winter fun!

Imitate a Native custom by planning a **Community Games Event** during the coldest days of Winter. These games are a sure way to bring out the warming smiles that will cure cabin fever!

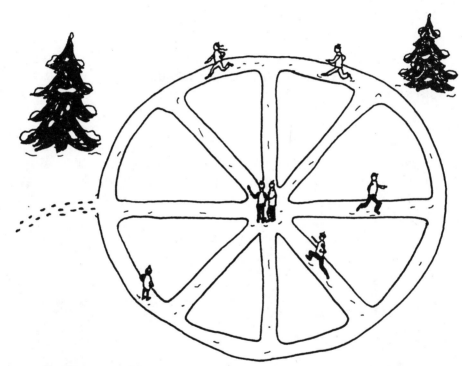

Fox and Geese ❧

1) Outside, make a large circle ten to twelve feet in diameter by dragging your feet through the snow. (How can you use your body parts to measure ten to twelve feet?) Drag your feet down the center of the circle, dividing it in half. If you cut the circle in half again, what do you have? If you cut each of the quarters in half, what do you have? Do you think you need to divide the circle smaller than eighths?

(continued)

2) In the very center of the circle, drag your feet to create a safety circle large enough to hold one or two geese at a time. Now it's time to choose a fox from the players. The remaining players are geese. You can probably guess what happens next! The fox tries to catch a goose. During the chase, all players must remain on the paths. The center is a safety zone, but no goose can stay there longer than three goose honks worth of rest, then the goose is off again! Remember that only one or two geese can fit into the rest area at a time. Other geese must keep on the move or they'll be caught by the fox.

3) Of course, the fox never stops until it catches a goose. Then the goose becomes a fox, and the fox becomes a goose. Or, instead of switching, foxes can increase until they outnumber the geese - which is what really happens when foxes are fattened by eating many a goose!

Tug o' Winter ❧

With this game, the Inuit people introduce lightheartedness and joy into the months of winter doldrums. Play the Tug o' Winter game with a lot of people who are tired of Winter.

1) Have all the ducks (people born in Summer and Spring) line up on one side of a Tug o' Winter rope. Have all the ptarmigans (those whose birthdays are in the Fall or Winter) line up on the other side of the rope. Tug o' Winter! If the ducks win, the Winter will be fair and mild. If the ptarmigans win, better get toasty warm and prepare for a long, cold Winter!

Winter Camouflage Trail ❧

1) Camouflage pictures of animals - such as deer, snowshoe rabbits, snow fleas, etc. - along a nature trail and invite others to find as many as they can. You might also enjoy hiding objects like pine cones, acorns, snow balls, or pussy willows.

WHERE HAVE ALL THE FLOWERS GONE?
DRIED FLOWERS

Those beautiful wildflowers you enjoyed all Summer now stand as delicate skeletal forms in the meadow. You can learn to identify them by the way they hold their dried seed heads, by their leaves and stems, even by their gestures. Spend some time getting to know a plant through its silhouette. Ask a wildflower silhouette some questions. Perhaps the answers will appear like magic as you sit quietly, observing, reflecting and listening.

&❧ One sunny, winter day you may find yourself in a meadow. Does a **dried wildflower or grass specimen** seem to be calling especially to you? If so, take a few minutes to visit your new meadow friend.

    ✿ What are its most interesting characteristics?
    ✿ Is it the shape of the dried seed and flower?
    ✿ The leaf arrangement?
    ✿ The kind of fruit?

🐌 If you spend some time trying to **discover the hidden mysteries of plants**, you might learn where they prefer to live, how they hold themselves upon the Earth, and how their gesture is unlike any other plant - as though they wished to tell you the story of their life! How many plants do you see in your daily life whose name you do not know? Do you need to know what to call them to appreciate them? Or do you simply appreciate their qualities and enjoy holding them in your memory?

🐌 **Take a close look at the flower.** What do you see? Here are some helpful hints and questions for getting to know a plant by its Winter dress.

Black-eyed Susan

- Is the flower umbrella-shaped?
- Are there any fruits or seed pods?
- How are the flowers arranged?
- Are they opposite?
- Are they spread along a spike?
- Do they grow in a cluster?
- Do they whorl around the stem?

Sometimes the shape of the dried plant may remind you of a blossoming wildflower friend of Summer. Can you imagine the bees and butterflies gathering nectar here? What might its color be when in full bloom? Look closely and try to imagine its special qualities.

🐌 **What happens when you crush a small section of the stem, flower, root, or leaves?** Do you detect an odor?

♠ If it smells like mint, then most likely you've found a member of the **Mint** family. Check for a square stem to be sure!

♠ Does it smell like carrots or parsley? Then you've found a member of the wild **Parsley** family. An umbrella-like flower shape is another clue that it belongs to the parsley family.

♠ How about a smoky smell? Then it's probably from **Daisy's** family.

🌿 **Did you look at the leaves?** Leaves can tell a lot about a plant, even if they are shriveled - or missing!

♠ Are they the wrap-around type? If so, most likely you've found members of the **Buckwheat** or **Parsley** family.

♠ Opposite leaves? Then you've met a **Mint** or **Pink** family member. Gently unfold some dried leaves along the stem and look at their shape.

opposite leaves

🌿 **Did you notice the wildflower's habitat?** Does it have shallow roots and live on a rock? Is it found beneath a tree? Does it prefer open spaces, such as sunshine-filled meadows? Look for more of the species, and when you find them check for clues to determine their desired habitat. Have you ever seen these plants blooming in other places? Flower families often share similar characteristics. As you wander through their territory, you may begin to notice some of their similarities.

✍ **Can you draw the silhouette of your new meadow friend in your journal**? Did you answer any of your questions during the drawing? Imagine this meadow friend in all its summer glory, then try to draw it. Write a poem or story about what you think its silhouette is trying to tell you.

🐦 With the aid of ***Weeds in Winter*** by Lauren Brown, you might enjoy keying dried wildflower specimens. Consider your experience studying winter wildflowers in the meadow. How did that experience compare to keying silhouettes from a book? Which experience made you feel most like an *active* learner, observing, questioning and drawing conclusions?

Want To Do More?

🐦 You can **make beautiful scenes** in the cradle of dried milkweed pods!

Milkweed Pod Ornaments

1) For a colorful lining, gently glue colored tissue paper or thin felt inside the pod.
2) Add tiny colorful dried flowers, sequin stars, or glitter.
3) Glue a thin, gold cotton crochet thread around the outside rim of the milkweed pod. Knot the cotton at the top so you can hang it. T

These make lovely ornaments. Put them on nature tables, or hang them in a window. Or affix them to a mobile made of a branch that has interesting bark.

Math, Nature's Way!

🐦 Look at a plant closely to discover if it is "unique". Just as no two people are <u>exactly</u> alike, neither are plants. But plants may

alternate leaves

have very **similar patterns**. Look closely at the way the leaves form around the stem. Do you see a pattern? Are the leaves *opposite, alternate,* or *whorled* around the stem? Try to draw the patterns for opposite, alternate, and whorled. If you find drawing the patterns to be a challenge, cut out six or eight leaves and a stem for each of the three patterns. Like a puzzle, place the leaves along the stem and glue them in place. Create each of the following patterns: opposite, alternate and whorled.

Now look at plants for a pattern known as **symmetry**. A plant has a "symmetrical" design if one half of the plant mirrors the other half. Draw one half (a right or left side) of a plant in your journal. Can you draw the other half of the plant so that the plant looks symmetrical?

🐛 Bring in a **milkweed** bursting with seeds. Empty the seeds into a glass jar and **try to estimate the number of seeds**! Count them out by 2's, 4's, 5's, 7's, 10's. How does your estimate compare?

whorled leaves

WINTER WILDFLOWER DISPLAY

One good way to remember your winter Meadow-Thicket plant friends is to bring them indoors. Make a display of the plants you find, as well as drawings and notes about each plant.

 You can design a **Winter Wildflower Bulletin Board** to display wildflower stalks. Hang the bulletin board at your EARS station or indoors.

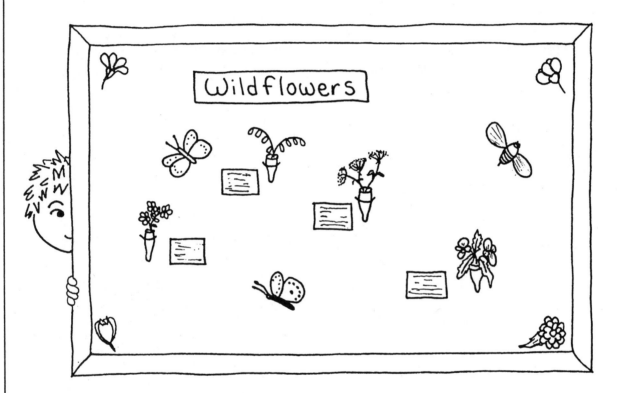

You will need:

a bulletin board
plastic florist vials
paper or felt

❧ Here are some ideas to get you started:

1) To hold these wonderful winter weed stalks in place, use recycled plastic vials, which florists often attach to the stems of roses and orchids. Or design paper or felt pockets. Attach these to your bulletin board.

2) Next to the winter weed, hang a detailed drawing of the plant in full bloom. _Golden Guides_ have good illustrations of plants, but you might prefer to create beautiful, hand-drawn art for your display.

3) Are there special winter identification characteristics you'd like to list alongside each stalk?

4) Save some empty vials for displaying future finds during the long winter months.

When you leave home for visits during the winter holidays, it's fun to bring back unknown specimens to display as mystery guests!

Want To Do More?

❧ Make **Holiday Bouquets** from dry wildflowers:

You will need:

decorated cans or glass bottles
gold spray or glitter
moss

1) Gather interesting dried wildflowers and scatter the seeds on the earth.

2) Arrange wildflowers in recycled, decorated, tin cans or glass bottles.

3) Add gold spray paint and/or glitter to your wildflowers, or preserve them in their naturally beautiful state.

4) Place moss around the stems of your wildflower arrangement.

5) Tie a festive bow to top off the arrangement!

Wildflower bouquets make lovely gifts for family members or community elders.

INDOOR WINTER GARDENING

Where have all the flowers gone? Remember the Day Lilies' lovely, orange trumpets, which bloomed all Summer long in the meadow or along the roadside? How does the mother plant continue to live from season to season? How do wildflowers survive in Winter? Force some bulbs indoors to learn about wildflower survival.

Have you noticed any signs of the Day Lilies' existence during Winter? Look for long, brown leaves, for tall stalks, for stems that once sprouted petals that trumpeted to the sun. Although each lily blossomed for only one day, the mother plant lives as a **perennial** on the meadow and roadside edge. Year after year, the tall stalk and greens of the mother plant rise toward the sun with yet another colorful family of trumpets to celebrate the summer days.

🐾 To learn about flowering perennials, force an **Amaryllis** bulb indoors. Since the Amaryllis plant is so large, it often seems to grow inches a day before your very eyes! This makes an Amaryllis especially exciting to watch and care for. It also provides lots of opportunities for graphing and charting amazingly rapid plant growth.

Force an Amaryllis Bulb

You will need:
an Amaryllis bulb
a clay pot
small stones
potting soil

1) Place a few small stones at the bottom of a clay pot to provide drainage.
2) Then add potting soil.
3) Position the Amaryllis bulb so that its top is even with the surface of the soil.
4) Add water, say "Abra Cadabra" and watch what happens!

♠ Pay attention to the leaves, stem, bud and blossom of the Amaryllis as the plant grows. You will probably notice little change during the first two weeks. But in the fifth or sixth week you will see a lot of growing and blooming activity. Every day, **measure** the growth of different plant parts and mark these on your plant growth chart. Are you surprised at what you find?

🐾 Where do you think an Amaryllis gets all the energy it needs to grow? The large Amaryllis **bulb** stores food for the plant. Before you placed the Amaryllis in a warm place and began to provide water, it was lying **dormant**, or resting. Unlike many other plants, an Amaryllis rests in all seasons but Winter. Each Winter the Amaryllis bulb goes through a period of growth and food production, then its greens die back.

🐾 Dormancy occurs at the end of its growth cycle. During this period, store the bulb in its pot of soil in a cool area where it will not freeze. During dormancy, the large bulb stores the energy it made during its last period of greening. Next Winter, bring it into your room to receive the warmth and water that will encourage a new cycle of blossoming.

How does the life cycle of a **Day Lily** plant compare to the Amaryllis? Day Lily plants have a fleshy, **tuber-like root**. This fleshy root system enables the Day Lily to store food for the following year. Since the root is planted deep in the soil, the earth insulates it from the cold. Winter snows provide an additional blanket of protection against the freezing cold. Other spring bulbs, such as tulips, store food underground in their bulbs each Winter, enabling the plant to rise year after year to the warmth of the Spring.

Want To Do More?

Other varieties of bulbs that can be forced indoors are narcissus, tulips, crocus, and mini-Iris. These make wonderful gifts for local elders.

"THE BUTTERFLY GARDEN"

Grandforest Tree speaks of fairies and elves:

Let me tell you what happened to a little boy and girl who used to play in my branches and swing on a tire swing from Spring to Fall.

"It began one late winter afternoon, after two straight days of raining and freezing weather. Ginny and Jason were bored beyond words. They had read and re-read all their books, played with their toys, and drawn endless pictures of Spring coming to the farm. Restless, Ginny began watering her mother's flowering house plants, when she thought she heard a whisper.

"'Pssssst! Hey, kid - come here!'

"The sound seemed to be coming from the Geranium, which sat on the windowsill and was, as always, in full bloom. Ginny stared at the blossoms in disbelief. The voice spoke again, this time a little friendlier.

"'Don't be frightened. I'm just a Flower Fairy. Thank you for watering us, we were very thirsty.'

"'Hey, Jason,' Ginny called excitedly to her brother, 'come listen to this!' Jason hurried over to Ginny, who bent over a Geranium, as the voice spoke again.

"'Hello, my name is Jahnessa. I'm the Fairy of this particular Geranium blossom. There are many more of us - one for each blossom. We've been watching you two for some time, and think you're perfect for a special project we have in mind.'

"'Check it out!' exclaimed Jason. 'Wait till I tell the kids in school! I think I'll bring it to my class and show everybody.'

"'Oh, please don't do that,' Jahnessa said. 'There are so few of us left! We're like an endangered species - if you take us outside this time of year, we might freeze to death!

Then we would become extinct.'

"Ginny and Jason had learned about extinct and endangered species in their ecology class. 'Oh, dear,' said Ginny, frowning. 'We wouldn't want that to happen. But why are there so few of you left?'

"The Flower Fairy told the two children that, long ago, a Fairy or Elf lived in every flower blossom. But when humans began cutting down the forests and creating fields, and then cutting the fields for hay, fewer flowers were able to bloom. As a result, she said, today there aren't as many Fairies or Elves - and their populations are becoming critically low.

"'Is there anything we can do to help?' asked Jason, still feeling guilty for his idea of taking the talking plant to school.

"'Well, yes - remember the special project I mentioned? We would love it if you would plant a flower garden this Spring. But not just any old flower garden. This one must attract butterflies, because Elves need butterflies to get around. We fairies have our own wings.' Jahnessa flew up from the blossom, showing them her flying skills.

"'Also,' she went on, 'butterflies help spread flowers around - just as bees do. But the Elves can't ride bees because bees are very busy and never seem to have time to transport the Elves anywhere.' The Flower Fairy paused, then asked with a smile: 'Would you like to plant a butterfly garden?'

"'Oh, yes, that would be wonderful!' the two children exclaimed. 'How do we start?'

"As the Fairy gave them some suggestions as to how to begin, it became clear to the children that they would need to do some research and careful planning before presenting the idea to their parents.

"But in the end their parents agreed, and the two children planted a successful garden, which flourished year after year - I can still remember how hard those two those two kids worked!

"Of course, all this happened many, many years ago. Today those kids are grown up and have moved away - no one has tended the garden for quite awhile. But although many of the plants have gone wild, the Fairies and Elves continue to dwell happily.

And that warms my heartwood - to see those little creatures flitting and fluttering around."

Would you like to plan a Butterfly Garden like the one Grandforest Tree spoke of? Just turn to the next activity to find out what to do!

THE BUTTERFLY GARDEN PROJECT

When seed catalogs begin filling your mailbox in February, it's difficult to wait until Spring to start thinking about gardening. Plan a Spring Butterfly Garden Project for your neighborhood and order seeds now! You might adopt a community elder to give this project intergenerational sparks.

Planting a Butterfly Garden, planting trees, or gardening in your backyard are examples of **habitat enhancement projects**. Habitat enhancement projects seek out areas that have been changed from their natural habitats to lawns or parks - in a sense they have been "domesticated". Habitat projects attempt to return them to their original state of existence so that they can become, once again, a natural habitat of wild plants, insects and wildlife.

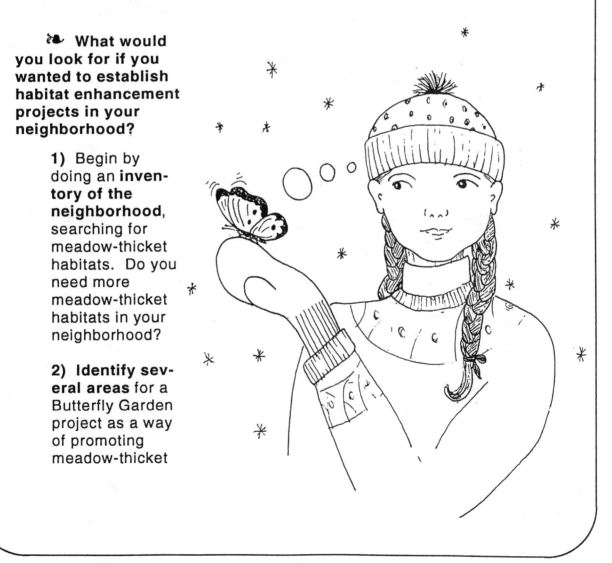

🐌 **What would you look for if you wanted to establish habitat enhancement projects in your neighborhood?**

1) Begin by doing an **inventory of the neighborhood**, searching for meadow-thicket habitats. Do you need more meadow-thicket habitats in your neighborhood?

2) Identify several areas for a Butterfly Garden project as a way of promoting meadow-thicket communities. Some suggestions include:

- **Lawn areas** around the school or other municipal buildings that could be allowed to remain natural.
- **Park edges** that could be planted as wildflower meadow-thicket areas for the entire community.
- Areas of **home lawns and gardens** that could be devoted to habitat enhancement.
- **Senior housing green areas** or **abandoned vacant lots** that could be renovated for a meadow-thicket project.

3) Research plants in your area that attract birds and favor nectar-collecting butterflies. You can begin by reminiscing about your favorite summer and autumn butterfly species.

- Which wildflowers are native to your state?
- What is your state flower? Why was it chosen?
- What types of naturally-occurring foods do local birds or butterflies enjoy?
- Among the recommendations in your Butterfly Garden habitat enhancement project, include several plant suggestions.

4) You might find useful information in seed catalogues, as well as in insect guides, or in books that describe bird and butterfly habitats. A helpful book by Barbara Damrosch, _Theme Gardens_, addresses ways to plan, plant and grow butterfly theme gardens.

🦋 **Organize a proposal for a Butterfly Garden** project in your neighborhood so that others can experience some of the winter wonders you've discovered in the meadow. Ten steps to get started are:

1) List all the benefits of a Butterfly Garden habitat enhancement project.

2) Make recommendations for kinds of plants and the amount of land necessary for the planting.

3) Determine who will manage and maintain the butterfly theme garden project (which includes fund raising, land preparation, getting the necessary approval, cultivating and maintaining the plantings).

4) Set the date for a community work day and advertise the Butterfly Garden campaign in your neighborhood.

5) Invite the local elders.

6) Ask someone to take photos for a newsletter.

7) Ask someone else to dedicate the project.

8) Plant a sign in the garden for posterity!

9) Lead meadow tours when the flowers mature.

10) Build public relations by calling the local paper.

For the Future:

If habitat enhancement projects like the Butterfly Garden seem to be well-received in your area, **fundraise** in advance for similar projects by selling Butterfly Garden Seed Collections. Seed suggestions might include Cosmos, Wild Asters and Cone flowers.

FOR THE BIRDS: BUILD YOUR OWN WINTER FEEDERS

Bird feeders near a window can inspire interest in the daily winter life of birds. Through careful observation, you can begin to learn their identities and characteristics.

🐦 Because the bird feeder is so close to the window, however, you may find it necessary to create a camouflaged bird blind so as not to scare the birds away. A screen of ferns or leaves taped to the window will enable you to see the birds without them being aware of you. You can also make a screen by covering the window with a tissue paper collage decorated as a shrubby forest scene.

🐦 Construct simple bird feeders from the suggestions below, or refer to the Nature Cafe activities for ideas. Covered bird feeders help keep food visible, dry, and available after snowfalls.

BIRDS OF A FEATHER
I.D. CENTER

What a pleasure it is to make a handy identification pouch, which can be hung near the bird-feeding window. Use it to keep track of who's who at the feeder. Make one for your own use, and another as a fundraiser for bird projects.

🐦 A bird identification center is easy to make if you follow the suggestions below. The idea is to sew several pockets and a pouch onto a large piece of burlap fabric which can hold bird I.D. cards.

You will need:

a needle and thread
a large piece of burlap
Golden Guide to Birds
scissors
glue
3 x 5 cards
clear shelf tape
markers

1) Make **bird identification cards** that will fit in the pouch pockets. You can draw the birds yourself, or glue pictures from an identification book onto the cards. Both the _Golden Guide to Birds_ and the _Audubon Pocket Guide_ work well for this. Laminate the cards with clear shelf tape to protect them. If you would rather draw birds, refer to the _Golden Guide_, noting upper and lower body color for a true-to-life representation.

2) Set up your Bird Identification Center near a window that looks out on a bird feeder. When you see a bird at the feeder, record the sighting by placing a card in the pocket.

Math, Nature's Way

❧ Post a **tally sheet** near the identification pouch to keep track of your daily observations. Display your final data on a **graph**. The data may answer some of the following questions: Which birds do you see most often at the feeder? Which visitors are the most unusual? Do more males or females come to feed? Is there a pattern to the time of day when the birds come to feed?

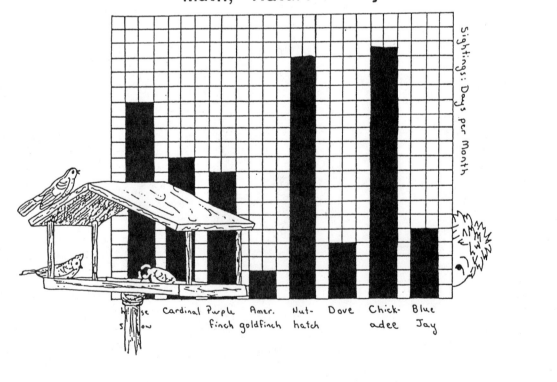

Math, Nature's Way

THE BEAUTY OF BIRDS: PARTS OF A BIRD

Setting up a bird feeding station is a great way to spend time with our winter feathered friends. When one of these friends lands at the feeder, watch it for as long as you can.

🐦 See if you can identify the parts of each bird, including:

♥ Do the male and female of each species look alike?

♥ Do the special markings of individual birds serve a particular purpose?

♥ Can you draw the male and female bird markings of a particular wintering bird?

♥ Compare your drawing of the winter plumage of the above birds to photographs or drawings of their plumage in other seasons. What do you see?

♥ By observing and recording daily seed choices, you may discover many things.
   ❀ Which birds prefer which seeds?
   ❀ What types of beaks serve what function for eating?
   ❀ Draw a bird, with special attention to the beak, along with the seed or food of its choice.

♥ What do you notice about bird behaviors around the bird feeder?

♥ Do some birds seem to be working at nearby trees? What do you think they are doing?

♥ What sound does each bird make while it searches for food?

If you notice a blue and gray bird walking upside down in circles on the tree singing a single, nasal syllable, that's probably **Nuthatch** looking under the bark for insects. **Woodpecker** and **Chickadee** don't perform the same acrobatics, but they too are searching for fruits and insects on the trees.

Want To Do More?

🐦 Have you observed **adaptations** that help birds survive in Winter? For clues, look at beaks, winter plumage, feet, tail feathers and food choices.

🐦 Why is it important to feed birds in your neighborhood during the Winter? If you weren't feeding them, where might the birds find the food of their choice? What happens to the supply of natural food for birds during Winter?

"HOW THE BIRDS GOT THEIR WINGS"

Grandforest Tree tells a windy story:

One night many summers ago, long before this land was cleared, the winds came howling down the mountain through the forest. I was frightened until I began to listen to what the winds were saying. Here's the story that streamed along the river of breezes:

"There was time when the birds had no wings. They were forced to walk everywhere they went, up and down mountains and hillsides, through forests, around lakes and ponds, searching the ground for food. They were very jealous of the Fairies, who had been given the gift of flight by the Creator. And yet the Fairies were considered a delicacy by the birds, who would eat them whenever they could catch them.

"Over time the birds had developed some interesting adaptations to capture the Fairies, who resided in a variety of habitats. Many Fairies lived in flowers, but others lived in trees, under leaves, in the water, in mushrooms, or underground. So the birds had to be very clever in their adaptations - otherwise they would go hungry.

"And so it was that Hummingbird had a long, skinny beak that was perfect for extracting Fairies from tubular flowers. Woodpecker developed a shock-absorbent head full of a jelly-like substance, as well as a strong bill, which enabled it to seek out Fairies hidden beneath the tree bark. Duck had a soft, spoon-shaped beak that helped it scoop up unwary Water Fairies.

"And yet many Fairies managed to avoid capture by flying away when they heard the birds tramping through the forest towards them. Tramp, tramp, tramp. The rumbling sound gave the heavy-footed land birds away.

"One day, Hawk, chieftess of all the birds, was wandering through a bog, looking for mice and frogs. Suddenly she came upon a Fairy lying injured in a Pitcher plant. This was a surprise, because as a rule Fairies tended to avoid bogs, which are full of Fairy traps - like Pitcher Plants and Sundews. Though Hawk didn't know it, this particular Fairy was a Fairy Prince, who was destined to become King of all the Fairies. The little Fairy was obviously in a lot of pain, and Hawk forgot all about her hunger.

"'Oh, dear, what happened to you?' Hawk asked, concerned.

"The Prince of Fairies shrank from Hawk's beady eyes. All birds were his enemy, and here he lay, defenseless and in much pain.

"'Do not fear,' said Hawk. 'I see that you are injured. I will not harm you - please let me help.'

"Though wary, the Fairy Prince realized he had no choice but to trust Hawk. So he told Hawk that his home was in a grove of beautiful, blue flowers, which grew in a field far, far away, beyond the Great Wood.

"Hawk was familiar with the field because on many occasions she had hunted mice and Fairies there. Gently, she picked up the Fairy Prince and put him on her back.

"She ran swiftly across the bog and through the forest. By the time she arrived in the field she was out of breath. Upon spying Hawk, the Fairies who had been playing in the sunlight instantly disappeared into their secret hiding places. But when they began to realize they were not in danger, they crept out one by one to have a better look.

"Hawk carefully set the Fairy Prince on a toadstool. Cautiously, the King and Queen came forward to examine their son. Soon he was surrounded by the Healing Fairies. Hawk, forgotten in the commotion, started to walk away. Tramp, tramp.

"The Fairy Queen, noticing Hawk's departure, spoke up. 'Hawk, big sister, we are grateful for what you've done. To show our gratitude, we shall give you and all your bird sisters and brothers the gift of flight. But you must agree never again to eat Fairies. Instead, you can eat insects, green plants, and other tasty morsels which are more abundant than Fairies - and easier to catch.'

"Suddenly, wings sprouted from Hawk's sides. She stood transfixed. In the blink of an eye the wings were fully formed.

"Humbly, Hawk bowed to the Fairies, thanking them for such a wonderful gift. 'From this day forth we shall have peace between us,' she said, her voice cracking with emotion. 'Never again shall my fellow birds prey upon Fairies. We shall help each other when in need, and be friends forever more.'

"'So be it,' chorused the Fairies, and with a great rush of wings, Hawk soared skyward.

"And so that's the story the winds told me that summer night. It's quite a wonderful tale, because ever since then I've understood something about Hawk that used to escape me.

"I'll let you in on my little secret. Whenever you see Hawk circling a field, she's not only looking for mice, but also thanking the Fairies for the fantastic gift of flight!"

MAY WE ALL FLY LIKE EAGLES

People often imagine themselves soaring as freely as a bird in flight. Why are we so attracted to this notion, and how can we learn more about our feathered friends?

Long before the land in North America was partitioned by boundaries to form the United States, many Native nations revered the eagle, which seemed to soar effortlessly through the heavens, viewing all of creation below. This perspective from the heavens was considered to be a gift given by the Great Spirit to the eagle, so Native Americans considered it a blessing when they saw one soaring. For those fortunate enough to catch a glimpse of this great bird, the eagle inspired questions and reflections.

🦅 The following **Eagle Chant** inspires feelings of respect for the bird, which has been chosen to represent our nation, the United States.

May we all fly like eagles
Flying so high
Circling the universe
On wings of pure light
O witchi ti ti
Witchi ti o ho
O witchi ti ti
Witchi ti i o
Witchi ti i o

Witchi ti i o oh o

Gather in a circle and create movements to go with this echo song. For example, as you chant or sing "May we all fly like eagles", open, unfold and expand your "wings". To the words "flying so high", move your wings in an up and down motion. As you softly chant or sing "circling the universe on wings of pure light", turn in a sunwise, or clockwise, direction.

As you circle sunwise, hold your wings outward, slowly tipping your body from one side to the other. Flap your wings while you step to the rhythm of the chant. Gradually soften your voice as you sing the last few lines.

Some suggestions for reflection:

How do you feel when you see an eagle soaring through the sky?

Have you ever wished you could soar and move as effortlessly as the birds?

🐦 If you could choose to be any bird, what would you look like?

🐦 What might you eat and where might you take shelter?

🐦 What would the wintry Earth look like as you soar above her? You might enjoy drawing yourself as a feathered bird of flight. Share a story of your winter adventures with another bird lover.

🐦 Do you know how far an eagle can see? Two friends can try to guess the distance by acting out the roles of an eagle and a mouse. The eagle and mouse should stand far away from each other, representing the distance they think an eagle can see.

🐦 Native wisdom reminds us of the eagle's far-sighted vision. If an eagle could tell you what it sees upon the face of Mother Earth, what would it say? Can you draw the landscape from an eagle's perspective?

🐦 Native wisdom also speak of the eagle's gift of seeing into the future, of forming a vision for tomorrow. If the eagle spoke to you regarding its vision of the future, what might it say?

🐦 You might enjoy reading, then retelling the story of _Hawk I'm Your Brother_ by Byrd Baylor, which tells of a young boy's love for a hawk that longs for its freedom.

FLYING EXPERIMENTS

What would it be like to fly? How do birds fly? What is it about a bird's structure that allows it to swoop and soar high above the ground?

🐦 To find out more about **birds in flight**, design your own experiments, or try some of the following experiments.

You will need:

Experiment 1:   umbrellas

Experiment 2:   a pin
                  a feather

Experiment 3:   8 x 11 scrap paper

Experiment 4:   large scraps of fabric, such as cotton and wool
                  thread
                  a paper clip or a cork

♠ Experiment 1: How is an umbrella like a bird?

- Go outside on a windy day with an umbrella.
- What happens when the wind picks up?
- Which part of the umbrella catches more wind, the topside or the underside? Why do you think this happens?
- Do you think the curved surface of a bird wing acts the same way?

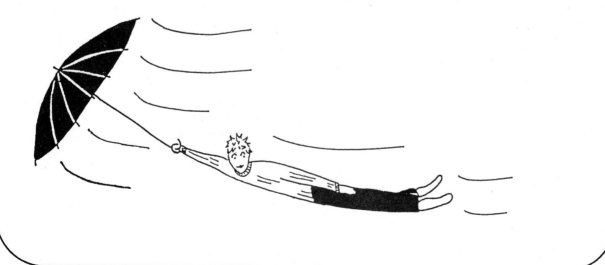

♠ Experiment 2: What happens when you blow on a feather?

Put a pin through the shaft of a feather. Holding the pin and feather firmly, point the feather straight out in front of your mouth. Now blow on the feather. Does the feather rise up? If so, why?

♠ Experiment 3: How is paper like a bird?

Drop a piece of paper from a height. What does it do? Try to design something from paper that sails through the air. Then make something that falls quickly to the ground. Which one is more like a bird in flight? What does the design of the "sailing" paper have in common with a bird?

♠ Experiment 4: How is a parachute like a bird?

Here's a parachute experiment that shows how curved bird wings promote flight and lift. Make a parachute from a square of fabric. Tie a thread onto each corner. Join the corner threads at the bottom by tying them to a paper clip or cork. Throw the parachute and observe what happens. How might the action of a parachute resemble a bird's wing?

Compare the flight capabilities of parachutes by making them different sizes and constructing them of different materials. Make six parachutes by cutting three squares of cotton and three squares of wool into 12", 8" and 4" pieces. Observe their flight patterns. What do you notice?

🐦 Did you know that birds have light, hollow bones, nearly weightless feathers, and streamlined bodies for excellent flight abilities? What do you think would happen if a bird's bones were thick and dense, and its wings weighty and large?

❧ While on a winter forest hike, **collect some feathers**. You might find some around the bird feeder. On city streets you can often find pigeon or seagull feathers. What do you see when you take a close-up look at these amazing structures?

❧ Have you ever noticed birds preening themselves - that is, smoothing or cleaning their feathers? Feathers are shaped to allow the wind to pass over them. You might notice that all the **barbs** - the tiny hair-like parts - are going in the same direction. Try to go against the grain or direction of the barbs by running your fingers along the feather. Does the feather look disheveled? When birds preen their feathers, they are actually *"zipping"* them into one direction. Can you *"zip"* the feathers back into their original shape? Look at a feather with a magnifying lens. Notice the tiny hooks that keep the feather zipped together.

EATIN' LIKE A BIRD

Did you ever notice how much time a bird spends eating during the Winter? What happens to your eating habits in Winter?

    🐦 Birds use an incredible amount of energy in Winter to keep warm. They need to eat constantly to fuel their tiny bodies. Did you ever notice that the more active you are on a cold day outside, the warmer you are? Or that you're really hungry when you come in after being outside for a long time? **Calories** are a way of counting how much energy your body needs. You need _an extra one thousand calories_ when you play outside on cold days.

    🐦 You probably know about **Go, Grow,** and **Glow foods.** "Go" foods give you energy, "Grow" foods, naturally, help you grow, and "Glow" foods help to keep you healthy.   What high energy foods - or _"Go"_ foods - do you like? Do these foods give you lots of pep? Some of them are better for your body than others. **Sugar** and **chocolate** make you go, but do not give you energy for very long. They are called **empty calories** because they contain no protein or vitamins - they don't build your body. Natural sugars found in **fruits** or **nuts** give you energy for a longer period of time, and also help build strong bodies by providing protein and vitamins.

(continued)

High Energy Snacks

Perhaps you'd like to make a high energy food snack to take along on your next outdoor winter discovery adventure. Make up your own combinations. Or try the following recipes, which are full of healthy *"Go"* foods.

🍎 Eatin'-Like-a-Bird Gorp 🍎

Make any combination of sunflower seeds, nuts, raisins, dates or other dried fruit, and Cheerios.

🍎 Zoom Balls 🍎

Combine peanut or almond butter, honey, dried milk powder, raisins and chopped dates. Roll the mixture into balls, then roll in shredded coconut or chopped nuts. These store well in the fridge or freezer until you need them. Yum!

🐦 What *Go* foods are good for birds? Suet, insects, seeds, corn and millet.

🐦 As you eat these delicious Eatin'-Like-a-Bird treats, think about this: Have you ever heard people say, "You eat like a bird"? What do you think they mean? What do you think "eatin' like a bird" means?

SCOOPER, SKEWER, NUTCRACKER, OR SIEVE?

Bird beaks are fascinating. Each bird has a unique beak, especially suited for the kind of food it eats. Are different kinds of beaks like different kinds of tools?

🐦 Display pictures of birds in their different habitats, along with enlarged pictures of their beaks.

❀ What food might each beak be suited for?

❀ How does the beak help the bird gather and eat food?

🐦 **To demonstrate birds' food gathering techniques, compare kitchen utensils to bird beaks!**

You will need:

a strainer
a nutcracker
a shishkabob skewer
a bottle opener
a spoon

1) Decide which kitchen tool represents which beak for each bird. Why does this tool best suit the bird? *(continued)*

2) Set out bowls of nuts and seeds (such as sunflowers, beech nuts, dried corn, or millet), tree bark, insects sandwiched between leaves, or leaves floating in a bowl of water. Explore ways of gathering each of these foods with the kitchen tools mentioned above. If a bird eats leaf and insect soup, what kind of beak might it have? What kind of beak would help a bird find food inside rocks? Can you design a new adaptation that could perform the task better or differently?

⧉ You probably remember that **survivors** are those animals most able to protect and care for themselves. Every animal has **adaptations** specific to its habitat and the food it eats. What is an adaptation? Can you describe the adaptations of some of your favorite birds?

Want To Do More?

⧉ Try this challenge. Create an imaginary bird out of paper mache, paying special attention to its beak. Now try to guess - based on the beak you've created - the bird's diet. Share your bird with someone, explaining its unique adaptations.

FLYING FEATHERS!
WHAT WAS THAT?

Observing birds at the feeder is very rewarding. After awhile you'll be able to identify birds by their silhouettes as they fly or perch on trees.

Here are three ways to make silhouette identification fun.

Silhouette Identification

You will need:

♥ **Flying Feathers!**
  black poster board
  straws or paper clips
  nylon fishing line
  scissors
  tape

♥ **Bird Mobile**
  bird silhouettes
  white paper
  crayons or paints
  a branch
  thread

♥ **Bird Silhouette Game**
  bird silhouettes

♥ Flying Feathers!

1) Using black poster board, cut out silhouettes of wintering birds in flight.
2) Tape a paper clip upright, or a drinking straw horizontally, across the back of each silhouette.
3) Suspend a string across the room at a gentle, sloping angle.

4) Slip the string through the paper clip or the straw, and let go of your bird silhouette! Whoosh! Watch the bird you made fly across the room. Ask someone to try to identify it before it lands!

♥ Bird Mobile

&❧ Make a **Bird Mobile** by hanging bird silhouettes from a branch.

1) Copy bird silhouettes onto <u>white</u> paper. Check your memory or a *Golden Guide Book* for details regarding the birds' features and the colors of its feathers. Remember to note what the bird looks like from above as well as from below. Crayons or paint will give your bird plenty of lifelike color.

2) Find an interesting branch, then suspend each bird silhouette from a thread so that it balances on the mobile.

3) Hang the mobile in a window to help you identify birds, or give the mobile as a gift to a bird lovin' friend.

♥ Bird Silhouette Game

&❧ As a culminating bird identification project, you might enjoy cutting out bird silhouettes of the major winter feeders. It's fun to cut out these silhouettes from black paper and display them on windows near the bird feeders. To check your bird identification skills, tape the name of the bird on the underside of the bird silhouette. Guess the silhouette, then check the answer hidden beneath.

A BIRD IN THE HAND:
NATURE NED THE SCARECROW

Nature Ned is a friendly fellow who loves to feed the birds each day - from his hand! Watch Nature Ned work his magic, then secretly trade places with him and see what happens!

You will need:
an outdoor chair
an old coat
gloves
an oversized hat
a tray
bird seed

1) Find a place outside that is easily observable from a window. Dress up a "Nature Ned" scarecrow in an old coat, gloves and an oversized hat. Set him outside on a chair with a cafeteria tray on his lap.

2) Fill his tray with bird seed. Watch as birds, and perhaps even squirrels, enjoy Ned's tasty treats! Keep a tally of all the hungry neighbors who feast there. It's unbelievable!

3) When the nature neighbors seem comfortable feeding from Ned's hands, it's time for you to go outside dressed in Nature Ned's cloak and hat. Sit down with the feeding tray on your lap, and stay still as a scarecrow! Friends can observe this memorable event from inside the building by standing very quietly at the window. Don't forget to take a photograph!

BIRD SEED GARDENING

Birds depend upon your conscientious efforts to supply bird seed in the Winter, but where do they eat the rest of the year? To discover what wild plants your bird neighbors eat during the growing season, germinate bird seed just before the Spring Equinox, March 21st.

You will need:

a flat cooking pan or wooden flat three inches deep
moist germinating mix
several varieties of bird seed
popsicle sticks
glue
a dark plastic bag

1) Fill a flat cooking pan or wooden flat three inches deep with moist germinating mix. Plant each type of bird seed in its own separate row. Planting depth should be four times the width of the seed. Be sure to count the number of seeds you plant in each row, and record this amount on a chart.

2) Mark each row with a popsicle stick, then glue a seed to the stick to identify the seed planted in that row.

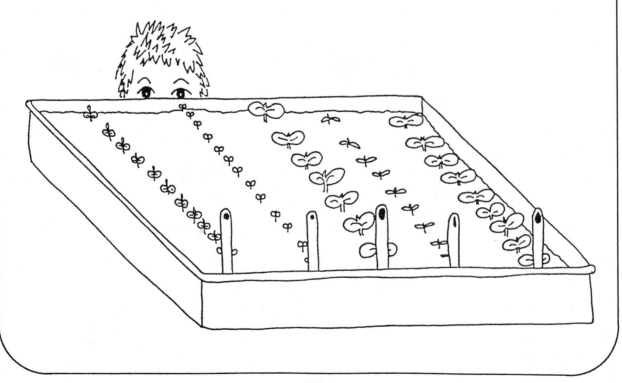

3) Cover the germinating tray with dark plastic to provide darkness and humidity.

4) Refer to the chart you made when you planted the seeds. For each kind of seed, estimate how many seeds you think will germinate. Now watch for emerging seedlings!

5) When most of the seedlings have emerged, count them and compare the number to your estimate. How close was your guess? Lots of other questions seem to pop up as quickly as the seedlings.

Can you answer these?
- Which seed had the highest germination rate?
- Which seed was the poorest germinator?
- Can you think of a reason why some kinds of seeds germinated more than others?

Observations:

- Which seed was the fastest to germinate? The slowest to germinate?
- Which seeds germinated the most? The least?
- Can you recognize the plants emerging from each seed?
- Have you ever seen these plants growing naturally outdoors?
- Illustrate the first emerging leaves for each type of bird seed planted.
- Illustrate the first set of true leaves for each type of seed planted.
- If the plants grow too large for the germinating flat, transplant them to larger, deeper containers, such as recycled milk cartons.

6) As the last spring frost approaches, acclimate the transplants to the sun, wind, and changing temperatures by placing them outdoors a few hours a day for three days. Next, leave them out overnight for three days. This will help them harden off. After the last frost, transplant your bird feed garden to a spot outdoors where it can grow to maturity and produce seed for the birds.

Want To Do More?

- Plant some of your sprouted bird feed gardens in a community

green, or put some outside an elder's window. This will enable other community members to observe birds feeding throughout the year.

 In the late Spring, try to identify some of the bird-feeding plants that grow naturally around your neighborhood.

HIAWATHA'S CHICKENS

"Then the little Hiawatha,
Learned of every bird its language,
Learned their names and all their secrets,
How they built their nests in summer,
Where they hid themselves in winter,
Talked with them whene'er he met them,
Called them "Hiawatha's Chickens".

by H. W. Longfellow

Now that you've had several opportunities to observe birds in a variety of activities, you're probably very familiar with your bird neighbors and are ready to write your own book of poetry! Try writing your own version of "Hiawatha's Chickens".

🐦 Before you write your poems, here are some ideas you may want to think about, just as Hiawatha did:

♠ What are the bird songs you've learned to "speak" or recognize?

♠ In what ways do birds look different during Winter?

♠ How do different kinds of beaks gather different kinds of foods?

(continued)

161

♠ What bird secrets would you like to tell about?

♠ Have you observed any nests of wintering birds in the bare trees?

♠ What names would you give your special bird friends if you could name them?

🐦 Remember the nature journal you made? Make a book just like it for your "Hiawatha's Chickens" poem or other poetry.

Want To Do More?

🐦 **Learn the poem** of Hiawatha with a few friends, and share it with other bird-lover buddies.

🐦 **Memorize** the "Hiawatha's Chicken" poem you wrote so you can recite it to your friends or family.

🐦 **Challenge** your friends to guess the name of the bird you are describing in your poem by omitting its name whenever it is mentioned.

🐦 **Publish** a special copy of "Hiawatha's Chickens" to exhibit or to keep as a reference in the nature library.

BIRDS OF A FEATHER
FLOCK TOGETHER

How can your community become "birds of a feather that flock together"? Celebrate the rich and abundant bird population in your neighborhood by planning a Winter Bird Celebration Day.

   ❧ **Hold a workshop to make bird feeders.** Invite your neighbors to donate recyclable containers or wood scraps for the feeders. Everyone can share design ideas and take home her own feeder.

   ❧ You might like to organize a community **bulk bird seed purchase** to keep the feeders well stocked. Keep track of cost, quantity and other amounts for a **"Math, Nature's Way"** challenge.

   ❧ How about a **Winter bird count** to document the neighborhood bird population? Are there special species you can protect or attract to your area? Can you identify wild plants which attract or shelter particular species in your neighborhood? *(continued)*

🐦 **Share your wealth of information** with your neighbors. How can your neighbors contribute to supporting the neighborhood bird community?

🐦 Do you know anyone who can **imitate bird calls, or recognize and identify birds through their calls** without actually seeing them? Invite this person on a winter bird walk.

🐦 Plan a **Bird Habitat Enhancement Project** in your community. Identify areas that support bird populations. Are the areas protected? How can you increase bird habitat areas in your community? Research plants that will encourage bird populations to reside in your community. Next Spring, work with community elders and parents to plant species of bushes and flowers that will enhance the development of bird habitats.

🐦 **Create a "Council of Birds".** Make bird masks and speak for the birds. If birds could speak for themselves, what would they tell us about the world they know? What would the birds say about the environment? Their future? Tell this story to your community guests.

LIFE ON THE EDGE: A SUCCESSIONAL FLIP BOOK

All things in Nature are constantly in a state of flow, growth and change. The life of a meadow is simply a step in time, for eventually it will become a thicket and then a forest. This change is called "succession".

🌱 While walking outdoors on a winter day, head toward the border of an open meadow. Observe the types of bushes or trees that grow along the border. These plants are known as plants that **live on the edge** - the edge being the end of the meadow and the beginning of the forest.

Looking deeper into the forest, you will see the different kinds of trees and bushes that inhabit the forest. Are the trees and shrubs on the edge the same as those within the forest? What might be the reason for the difference? Do you think this land was always forest?

🌱 As already mentioned, when one habitat changes into another habitat, it is called "succession". You can get a glimpse of the future of the meadows of the Earth by **making a mylar flip chart book**, which produces an effect similar to time-lapse photography.

A Mylar Successional Meadow-Thicket Flip Book

you will need:

an observant eye
mylar
masking tape
permanent markers
thick cardboard or a three-ring binder
a hole punch
string or metal rings

A) Cut nine or ten mylar sheets the same size. Tape the edges of the mylar with plastic or masking tape to prevent cracking and tearing.

B) Cut a piece of thick cardboard two inches wider and two inches longer than the mylar pages. The cardboard is the final page and support for the mylar flip book.

C) Punch two or three holes for metal rings through the top of the cardboard, matching the holes at the top of the mylar pages. Or, instead of cardboard, use a three-ring binder to house the successional flip book pages.

☛ ***Before you begin drawing,*** *think about the changes you observed in the meadow during the various seasons, as well as the research you have done.*

D) Begin illustrating the various stages of succesion in the meadow-thicket by:

1) On the first (bottom) page of the overlay book, illustrate the foundation layer of the meadow, such as rocks, soil and the underworld beneath your feet.

2) What comes next? Stones covered with mosses and lichen? On the second page, which lies atop the first page, add lichen and mosses to the rocks you illustrated on the first page.

3) Now for some grasses. Draw them around the rocks on page three.

4) Are wildflowers squeezing up between the grasses? Are there any butterflies or bees? Draw these on page four.

5) Small shrubs begin to take root on the fifth page, which overlays the wildflower page. Mice, snakes, rabbits, hawks and other critters like living in this environment, so draw them too!

6) On page six, trees begin to find their way into the meadow. Some Staghorn Sumacs maybe? Deer move in, too.

7) Page seven. Beyond the Staghorn Sumac are sun-loving deciduous trees. Foxes, snails, and woodpeckers join the neighborhood.

8) Page eight. Evergreen trees and ferns grow in the shade of the deciduous nurse trees.

9) Page nine. Old trees are losing their branches. Mushrooms and fungus feast on these ancient trees.

E) Now, beginning from the first or bottom page, flip through the changing life of the meadow as it succeeds to a forest habitat.

Voilà, a walk through time!

IN THE THICK OF IT MUSEUM: A WINTER NATURE DISPLAY

Meadow life is truly active during the Winter. Set up a museum to demonstrate what you have discovered during your winter Ecology Action Research adventures.

A Winter Nature Museum

You will need:

a table
a large cardboard box
mural paper
paints and brushes
markers
meadow-thicket treasures

🐌 **Here are some suggestions to create your museum:**

♥ Beneath the table, make a cardboard **display of the below-ground burrows of animals who hibernate.** Door flaps could conceal pictures of each resident who hibernates underground. Do you remember what a hibernating animal does during the Winter? Why do they hibernate? You might want to record a mini-version of this display by making sketches in your journal.

♥ **Above ground, display nature items** you gathered during your visits to the winter Nature Neighborhood. Interesting things might include scat, pine cones, branches, dried mushrooms, galls, feathers, gnawed grasses or brush, dried wildflower stalks and seed pods. You can even make molds, casts or drawings of animal tracks. Temporarily, you can even display insect cocoons. (If you keep insect cocoons in a jar on ice, and return them to the refrigerator or outside after displaying them, it is possible to study them without harming them.)

♥ **In the upper levels you can display** old nests, silhouettes of wintering birds, snowflake crystal patterns, tree silhouettes, and even the starry night sky. What makes the winter sky special?

A Culminating Winter Celebration Project

❧ As part of a **culminating winter celebration project**, invite younger friends, classmates, parents or community elders on a:

♥ **Meadow-thicket nature tour.** Interpret the museum for your guests, and give outdoor nature tours. What winter mysteries have you discovered? Would you enjoy sharing these mysteries by telling a story or creating a riddle as you lead guests along the tour trail?

♥ You might even enjoy performing a **Winter Wonderland Play** for your community guests. Try making masks and dressing up as meadow-thicket inhabitants, then tell your story of the winter wonderlands through the voice of meadow characters. Simple masks can be made from felt or brown paper and elastic bands. Add felt ears, pipe cleaner whiskers, fake fur, wool fleece, or feathers. Face painting is another costume option.

♥ Make this event a friendly and playful winter celebration by putting aside some time for **meadow nature games and nature hunts**. Some games you can play have been described in "Nature Games in Winter", page 51.

Happy Winter!

SPRING

WELCOME TO SPRING!

The snow is melting, the days are growing longer, and the first birdsongs of spring are filling the air. If you look up, you might even see a flock of Canadian geese heading north! Spring wildflowers are beginning to peek up through the meadow grasses, and could that be a moth fluttering by? Can you smell the delicious fragrance of the Earth as she melts and softens and warms?

Spring is here, that exciting, exhilerating, intoxicating season that comes like a miracle each year. Put your hats, scarves, and mittens away, and grab your sneakers - and maybe an umbrella for those spring showers. Let's go outside to the Meadow-Thicket and watch the magic!

☛ *Note:* If you would like to learn about Ants (starting on page 206) and build the Ant Farm this Spring, now is the time to mail-order some ants from a company that specializes in Ant Farms. One reliable source is:

Insect Lore Products
P.O. Box 1535
Shafter, CA 93263

The company will send you a coupon so you can mail-order live ants. It will also supply you with an **Ant Replacement Kit**, which includes food for the ants. Since the coupon must be mailed to the company before you can receive the ants, remember to allow ample time for live ant shipping, which usually takes two to three weeks. If your Ant Farm won't be set up by the time the ants arrive, be sure to construct a temporary home for them.

You can order a pre-made, plastic Ant Farm from this company, or you can construct your own farm. In either case, plan ahead - be sure to have a farm ready before the ants arrive. Remember: live ants must be attended to immediately!

"OLD MAN WINTER MEETS SPRING"

Grandforest Tree tells a story about Old Man Winter meeting his match.

Long, long ago, all the world was covered with deep snow and great sheets of ice. Old Man Winter ruled the land. He ruled it day after day, year after year. His kingdom encircled the entire earth. It was a bitter cold, joyless place to be.

In the middle of this frozen world, where the snow was deepest and the ice at its thickest, Old Man Winter built his house. It was very large, made from blocks of snow and chunks of ice, and so cold inside that even Old Man Winter had to wear a robe. He had no friends, other than the wind and the cold, and he was glad to rule alone over his frozen, bleak kingdom.

But one day, as he was sitting in his icy throne eating a bowl of frost, he heard a terrible noise. It sounded like a chirp, a trill, a tweet. He rose in fury from his throne and blasted out the door to discover a small bird with a red breast sitting on the top of his house.

"Who are you?" demanded Old Man Winter, ice chilling his every word.

"I am Robin. Some call me Spring."

"Spring! Bah! There is no Spring in my land. Go away, foolish bird, and take your horrible noisemaking with you!" Glaring with cold, grey eyes at the small bird, Old Man Winter turned with a great flourish, swirling his silvery robe around him, and strode back inside his house, where he shut the door with a great slam!

"Hrmmph! Spring! Hah, ha, hah!" boomed Old Man Winter as he returned to his throne and his bowl of frost. "There is only ice and snow in my kingdom, and it shall be that way forever!"

A broad, evil smile spread across his face as he thought of the foolish bird freezing up on his roof. But then - splat! - a cold drop of water landed on the top of his head. Then - drip! - another. Old Man Winter spun in his throne and gazed up at his ceiling. There, at the very highest point, the ice was melting!

"Blizzards and tempests!" shouted Old Man Winter in a rage. "How can this be possible?"

Again he stormed out of his house. And again he saw the little red breasted bird atop the roof of his house, singing and chirping and tweeting. But this time the bird was sitting in the middle of a nest made from tiny grasses.

"Robin you fool!" shrilled Old Man Winter. "How dare you build a nest atop my house. Now I will unleash all my fury upon you!"

When Robin continued to sing and chirp, Old Man Winter gathered fists of snow and spears of ice and began to hurl them madly into the air. He bellowed and roared, shaking the entire earth with his icy blasts. The sky grew dark, the winds boiled and shrieked, and the snow drove down in blinding torrents.

"Spring, you are banished."

Laughing uproariously, Old Man Winter returned to his house and poured himself a glass of rime. "A toast to myself," he shouted, raising his goblet high. "Farewell, foolish Spring."

When Old Man Winter awoke the next morning, the terrible storm he unleashed had ended. The day dawned bright and clear. But as he lay in his bed, he saw that it was too bright - and too clear. Old Man Winter opened his eyes fully - and saw that most of his roof was gone! It had melted! And what was that awful, horrible noise? It sounded like thousands of birds chirping and singing and tweeting. He clapped his hands to his ears and stormed out of bed. Once again he raced outside. Birds nested everywhere he looked. And there, in the center of them all, was the Robin, with three blue eggs beneath her.

"You cannot stop Spring, you foolish old man," said the Robin. "I am keeping my eggs warm, and in so doing I am thawing your kingdom. See my friends? They have joined me,

and are warming their eggs in their nests. Look around, cold-hearted old man. Wherever the snow melts, green grass sprouts. And butterflies and bugs - and even a tiny fawn - play in the sun. It is you, old man, who is banished!"

As Robin spoke her last word, Old Man Winter's entire house collapsed. Before his very eyes, it became a sparkling, bubbling brook. The brook flowed out into the new meadow, bubbling its way south.

"You'd better head north, Old Man Winter. Spring is here - and you cannot stay. Go! Go quickly before you also melt!"

With one last, icy gasp Old Man Winter swung his silvery robe around him, and strode quickly in the direction of the far, far north.

Spring remained, and the land turned green and full and warm. Robin happily raised her small babies, chirping in the sunshine. The babies became three strong birds, who flew and soared and sang themselves.

When all the birds and bugs and animals were strong, some of them decided to take a long sleep, but others returned to the south to visit their homeland for a time. Being good-natured, they decided to let Old Man Winter return to his own land for awhile. But only for awhile. For Robin, who some call Spring, returns every year, ever since.

WALKING SOFTLY ON OUR EARTH:
SIGNS OF SPRING

Spring hikes are a wonderful time for observing seasonal changes and for learning to recognize Spring's life stirrings. By looking at the natural world with eyes of wonder and respect, you can develop an "insight" into new ways of perceiving Nature. Discover what it means to be a relative in the family of life. Experience a deep inner-connectedness to all living things. You might enjoy inviting a Native person or elder on this walk.

If you look into the natural world with the expectation of developing an inner eye or "insight" into the wonders of Mother Earth, hiking can be enjoyed in a different way. It helps to close your mind and open your heart - your inner eye - to the stirrings of the Earth.

Native People, as well as many of your elders, have acquired wisdom about the Earth both from the teachings of their elders and - more directly - from the Earth and her creatures. No textbooks or scientific methods are required to receive these teachings. The Native peoples considered the Earth to be their Mother, and all creatures her children. With an open heart and ear, you too can receive messages from Mother Earth. Have you ever felt yourself to be a special friend of Mother Earth?

❧ On your next hike, search the Earth for signs of new life. During Spring, there seems to be a great stirring within the Earth.

- Look for colors, smell fresh scents, listen for spring songs.
- Look for spring behaviors among the plant kingdom.
- Look for the no-legged, the two-legged, the four-legged, the six- and eight-legged creatures.
- Stop when something of interest calls to you. Sit quietly with it for a few moments. If you like, call your friends and share your discovery and its teachings.

❧ Here's something the Native American people have said, which you can carry in your heart. "Walk gently upon the Earth Mother in springtime, for she is pregnant."

- What does this mean to you?
- If the Earth is your Mother, then how should you treat her when you are hiking?
- If the Earth is your Mother and all creatures are her children, how might you be related to the Nature wonders you discover daily?

If you like to sing, try the following hiking song:

Deep Deep

We say it deep, deep
We say it down, down
We say it deep down in our hearts.
We say it deep, deep
We say it down, down
We say it deep down in our hearts.

We're trustees of this Sacred Earth
Deep down in our hearts.
We're trustees of this Sacred Earth
Deep down in our hearts.

(Repeat:)
We say it deep, deep.....

Unknown

178

The words to "Deep Deep" are easy to learn. *Children's Songs for a Friendly Planet,* by Evelyn Weiss, contains not only "Deep Deep" but also another good song called "The Earth is Our Mother". Two more songs, "My Roots Go Down" and "My Two Hands Hold the Earth" can be found in Sarah Pirtle's cassette *My Two Hands Hold the Earth.* Look up and listen to the words of these other songs and see if you can memorize them too!

🕊 After a wonderful outdoors experience with friends, a **closing share circle** provides a way of coming together to affirm, recognize and support new understandings and feelings. It's a great transition between activities because it centers and completes the past activity, preparing everyone for what lies ahead.

Try this Native-inspired share circle format, which helps people listen to one another when everyone has a lot of exciting news to share.

Pass a "talking piece" around the share circle. The talking piece may be a natural object such as a stick, rock, pine cone, or feather which you picked up during a hike. The person holding the talking piece is listened to by the entire group. When he finishes speaking, he passes the talking piece to the next person in the circle.

Want To Do More?

🕊 Draw posters of signs of Spring.

🕊 Draw pictures of the various wild places around your neighborhood that you would like to caretake or adopt. Draw yourself caring for these wild places.

🕊 What might be your commitments for living in harmony with these wild places? How can you live lightly and respectfully on the Earth? Write a poem expressing these commitments.

🕊 How does it feel to consider yourself a relative to all living beings?

SPRING EQUINOX: MYSTERY AND CELEBRATION

What is it about the relationship of the Earth and sun during Spring that causes life to stir? The Spring Equinox is a seasonal turning point when the length of day and night is equal. What is so important about this moment in time? How can we better understand and celebrate the Spring Equinox?

The following four **experiments** will help reveal the magic of the planets.

You will need:

 Solar Observations
washable crayon

 The Globe Experiment
a globe
a lamp
a flashlight
a map

 The Flashlight Experiment
a flashlight
2 sheets of paper
a pencil

 The Hand Lens Experiment
a glass hand lens
a piece of paper
a soaking wet sponge

❤ Solar Observations

How does the sun's position change as Spring turns to Summer?

Beginning on the Spring Equinox, March 21st, make daily observations of the sun for three months until the Summer Solstice arrives on June 23rd. Be sure to observe the sun's position in the sky from the same window at the same time each day. With a crayon, show the sun's position by drawing a yellow circle on the window. What do you notice about the angle of sunlight during this three month period?

❤ Globe Experiment

How does the sun's light make Winter and Summer, or day and night?

1) On a globe, find the place where you live. Now look for the Equator, the North Pole and the South pole. What do you notice about your location on the Earth? What do you notice about the tilt of the Earth?

2) To demonstrate the Earth's position relative to the sun during Spring, shine a lamp on the globe. Notice where the Earth's axis points.

3) Demonstrate the Earth spinning in its journey around the sun, but be sure to hold the globe so that the axis remains pointing in the proper direction. Remember: the Earth's axis never changes.

4) What do you notice about the way sunlight strikes the United States during the Spring Equinox? At this time, both poles receive the same amount of sunlight, which means that days and nights are equal the world over.

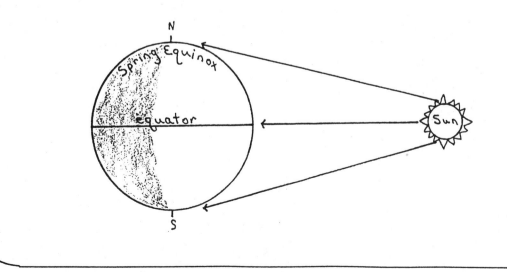

5) Demonstrate how the sun strikes the Earth during the Summer Solstice, the Autumnal Equinox, and the Winter Solstice. What do you notice about the angle of the sun's rays as they strike the Earth during each of these seasons?

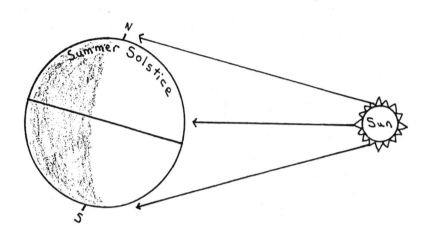

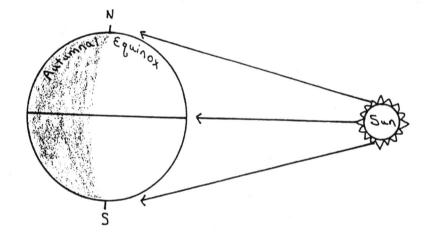

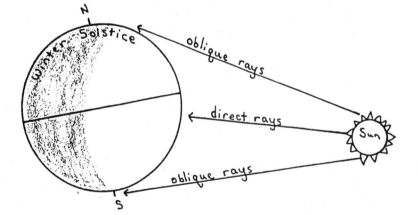

6) In the United States, which seasons get the most sunlight? Does it seem that on some occasions the sun's rays shine directly on the United States, but at other times they strike it at an angle?

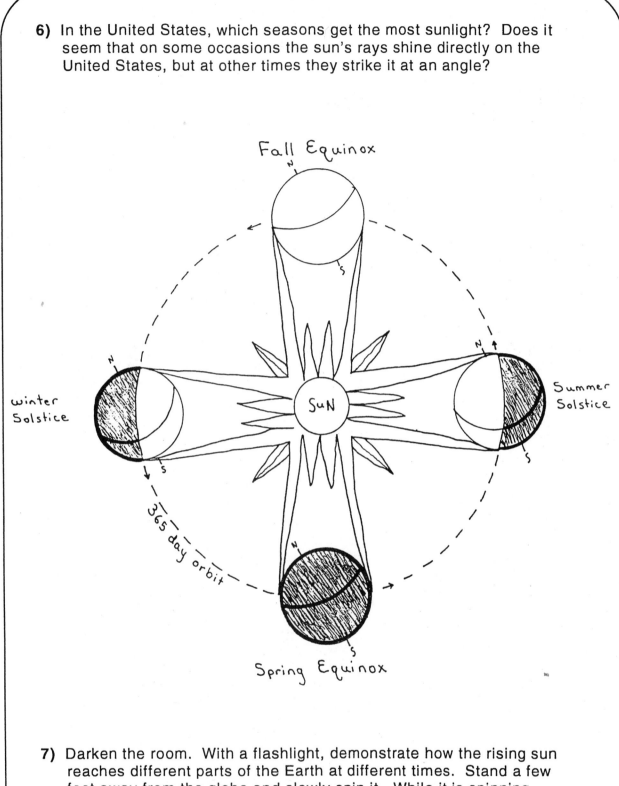

7) Darken the room. With a flashlight, demonstrate how the rising sun reaches different parts of the Earth at different times. Stand a few feet away from the globe and slowly spin it. While it is spinning, shine the flashlight on the globe. Notice how the light falls on the Earth. When dawn begins to creep over New York City, it is still dark in San Francisco. The people of many nations in Europe are sleeping when Americans are awake!

⬤ Flashlight Experiment

This next experiment will ask you to think about the difference between "straight on" sunlight and "angled" sunlight.

1) Have two pieces of paper, a pencil and a flashlight ready. Turn off the lights in the room. Now direct the light of the flashlight straight down onto a piece of paper. (Since you will be doing this again in a few minutes, memorize the distance between the paper and the flashlight.)

2) Trace the shape of the light pattern as it falls on the paper.

3) Next, hold the flashlight the same distance above the paper as before. But this time slant the flashlight so that the beam shines at an angle over the paper. Trace the shape of the light pattern as it falls on the paper. What do you notice about the shapes of the two light patterns on the paper? Why do you think this happened?

4) Repeat the experiment, this time shining the flashlight on your hand. Is there a difference in the strength of the light at different angles?

🍎 Hand Lens Experiment

Why does sunlight feel warmer at certain times than other times?

☛ *This experiment requires the supervision of an adult, and should be performed at noon.*

1) Hold a glass hand lens directly above a piece of paper, just as you did with the flashlight in the previous experiment. Allow the sun to shine through the hand lens onto the paper.

2) Move the lens up and down until the spot of light on the paper becomes very small and very bright. As the light burns into the paper, does the paper begin to smoke? Keep the sponge handy in case you need it!

3) Now hold the hand lens at an angle above the paper, as you did with the flashlight in the previous experiment. What happens to the strength of the heat or light this time?

4) Compare the results of this experiment with the results of the Globe experiment.
    ❀ Do you remember how the sun struck the Earth at different angles each season?
    ❀ Which is the coldest season? How does the sunlight strike the Earth at that time?
    ❀ What did you discover about sunlight during the spring season? Why would life stirrings begin in Spring?

🐚 What brings the flow of life back into the Earth Mother where you live? Think about the Earth's journey around our sun. When does the Earth tip ever closer to the sun's beneficial life rays? Was there a time today when you could feel the flow of life stirring inside you?

* Although there is only one sun for the entire planet, everyone gets some of it! What can we learn from the sun? What are some ways in which you can be like the sun? Do you share yourself? Do you cooperate with friends? Do you bring sunshine to those around you? Are you part of the rhythm and flow of Nature?

Math, Nature's Way

* Try some **solar math**. How do the hours of daylight change throughout the year? Use the chart below to create some interesting problems - and then try to solve them! What do you notice about the amount of increase or decrease in sunlight each day as the year progresses? Is the gain or loss the same each day, or does it vary from day to day and month to month?

DAY LENGTH CHART

SUNRISE AND SUNSET ON THE FIRST DAY OF EACH MONTH

(From Burlington, Vermont)

JANUARY		FEBRUARY		MARCH	
Rise	Set	Rise	Set	Rise	Set
7:29 am	4:23 pm	7:12 am	5:01	6:31 am	5:40 pm

APRIL		MAY		JUNE	
Rise	Set	Rise	Set	Rise	Set
5:34 am	6:20 pm	4:44 am	6:56 pm	4:11 am	7:30 pm

JULY		AUGUST		SEPTEMBER	
Rise	Set	Rise	Set	Rise	Set
4:11 am	7:41 pm	4:39 am	7:41 pm	5:15 am	6:30 pm

OCTOBER		NOVEMBER		DECEMBER	
Rise	Set	Rise	Set	Rise	Set
5:50 am	5:34 pm	6:30 am	4:42 pm	7:08 am	4:14 pm

Want To Do More?

❧ **What can you do to "bring out the sunshine" in those around you?** Plan a community service project. Distribute wildflower seeds to neighbors and assist them in establishing a wildflower garden on their land. Force bulbs indoors, then deliver them to a neighborhood elder who needs cheering. Sing some "Spring-y" songs while you visit, and share some tea and home baked goods.

❧ Design a **Spring Equinox Celebration** to acknowledge the gifts of Spring. Plant some of your own seeds of hope and promise, just as Spring plants her seeds of hope upon the land. Decorate the celebration area with "Signs of Spring" artwork and posters. Research songs, dances and rituals that you can share with guests invited from your community.

Golden Sun,
    light up our Earth,
        light up our skies,
            light up our hearts!

SPRING MEADOW WILDFLOWER HIKE

Spring is a wonderful time for observing plants that have emerged from their winter rest to decorate the landscape. Observe wildflowers while hiking in the meadow or along the forest edges.

🐌 Did you know that **Skunk Cabbage** gets its name from the rotten odor you smell when the plant is bruised? To find Skunk Cabbage, look in a wet or marshy area of woods adjoining the meadow. Skunk Cabbage sprouts very early in Spring, and actually melts the snow around it as it emerges. When emerging, it is large, purplish-brown and green-speckled, and shaped like a vase. Within this vase is a yellowish knob covered with tiny flowers. A Skunk Cabbage will grow a foot or two high.

Skunk Cabbage
1'-2'

❧ **False Hellebore** also gets an early start in Spring, though not nearly as early as Skunk Cabbage. Growing in meadows or wet wooded areas, the False Hellebore's yellow-green leaves are conspicuous in Spring, as is the plant's size. Its ribbed leaves resemble those of a corn plant. Eventually, a cluster of hairy, star-shaped flowers form at the top of the stalk. This plant is poisonous to eat!

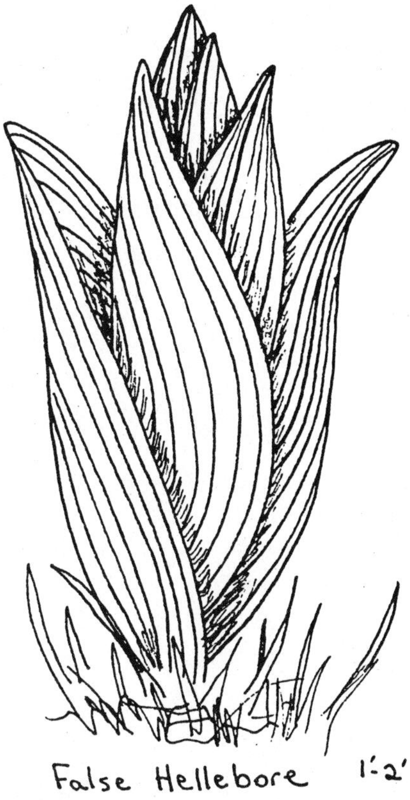

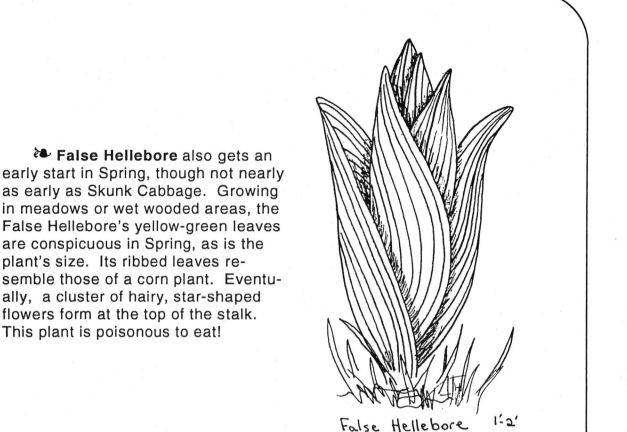

❧ "**Dandelion** will make you wise, tell me if she laughs or cries." Have you ever heard this saying? Dandelion actually gets its name from the shape of its leaf, which resembles lions' teeth. Examine one closely to see if you agree. Young dandelion greens make a nice addition to spring salads. Look for the yellow bloom that stands alone atop the stalk. As you hike around the spring meadow, see which critters are the first to visit dandelion flowers. If you break open a dandelion stem, what identifying characteristic do you find?

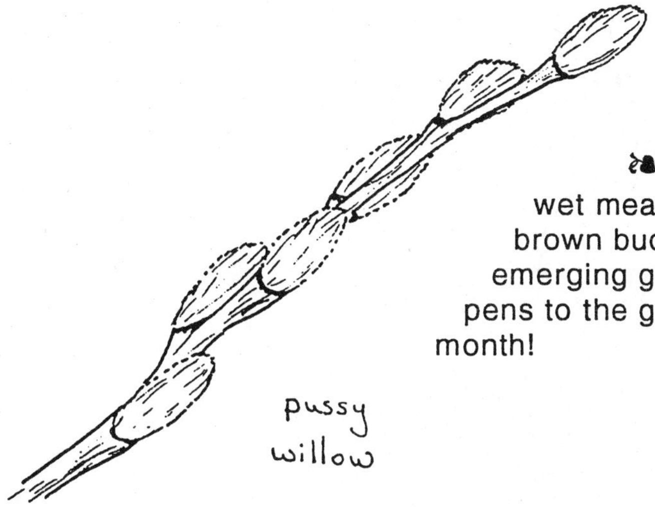

❧ **Pussy Willow** waits in the wet meadow for you. Observe the brown bud cases that protect the emerging gray fuzz. Watch what happens to the gray fuzz over the next month!

Cowslips, or Marsh Marigolds, are cheerful plants whose yellow blossoms poke above the wet meadow. Thick, green, heart-shaped leaves surround the bright blossoms, which are sometimes used to make a light-yellow plant dye. Look closely at the plant. Does it remind you of Buttercups? Why do you think these plants are named Marsh Marigold or Cowslips rather than Marsh Buttercups? Cowslips are edible, so boil the leaves and rinse them several times. Add vegetables for a wonderful spring soup.

You might enjoy packing a picnic lunch or a snack for the hike. What foods can you pack for health and extra energy? Remember to consider foods that help you to **Go, Grow, Glow.**

Marsh Marigold   12"

LIVING WILDFLOWER DISPLAY BULLETIN BOARD

A simple bulletin board can be constructed to display wildflower species you've collected. Gather specimens near your home or from a neighboring meadow. Since bulletin boards are a great way to display and identify species that may not grow in your Nature Neighborhood, gather specimens from a vacation spot. If you live in the city, you'll be surprised to learn how many wildflowers grow in lawns. Though less showy than their country cousins, wildflowers are abundant in urban areas.

(Remember: pick no more than one-third of a species from each location!)

You will need:
plastic vials from florists
poster board, wood, flannel board or bulletin board
clear contact paper
fresh wildflowers
flower press
construction paper
scissors
baby powder
pipe cleaners

❧ To create the wildflower display, hang a dozen small, plastic vials from a poster board, wood, flannel board or a bulletin board. These 3- or 4-inch plastic vials can be recycled (or purchased inexpensively) from a florist. Or, you can get them free when you buy roses, orchids, or other flowers from a florist.

❧ Place a wildflower in each vial. Remember to fill the vials with water daily to prevent the flowers from wilting.

❧ **Draw identification index cards** for each specimen and hang them beside the appropriate vial. Protect these cards by laminating them with clear Contact paper. Use the display to demonstrate any identification characteristics you want to emphasize, such as:

- Flower parts
- Square stem wildflowers
- Pistil and stamen formations that attract pollinators
- Opposite, alternating or whorled leaves
- Flower families

❧ After displaying the flowers for a few days, you can preserve them by pressing them in the flower press you made last fall.

❧ As an accompaniment to the display, cut out oversized plant flower parts from cardboard or construction paper. Cut out several petals, sepals, and leaves, as well as a stem, pistil, and stamen. These pieces may be used in different combinations to represent different species of wildflowers.

❧ Demonstrate a different wildflower each week by changing the display. It might be fun to add yellow tinted powder to the stamen to represent pollen. Powder can be tinted yellow by adding tumeric or curry powder to it. Or, corn meal makes nice "pollen" too. Make bees or butterflies. Hang them on the display by attaching them to the end of a pipe cleaner. Arrange them in such a way that they imitate the act of flower pollination.

The wildflower display can be placed anywhere you like - even in your Ecology Action Research Station!

Parts of a Plant Puzzle

If you look carefully at the different flowers of the Meadow-Thicket, you'll see that many of their parts are similar. Can you recognize what makes each plant unique?

Make a flower parts puzzle of the common plants found in your local Nature Neighborhood meadow. It's a real challenge to construct the individual parts of a plant neighbor! After several plant puzzles have been made, mix up the pieces, then piece each puzzle together by locating the proper plant parts.

You will need:

cardboard or poster board
scissors
enlarged examples of plant parts
crayons
a large plastic container

🐦 For each specimen you want to represent, cut puzzle parts from cardboard or a poster board. Check each plant carefully to make sure you cut out the proper shape and correct number of blossom petals. Follow the same procedure when you cut out the flower's sepals, stem and leaves. Color the pieces to resemble each specimen. Here are some questions to consider:

- What number and what shape petals does the nature neighbor have?
- Is its stem hairy, prickly, smooth, reddish, green?
- Are the edges of the leaves toothed, smooth, or lobed?
- Are the leaves opposite, alternate, or whorled?
- Can you name the plant parts as you piece them together?

🐦 Once you have cut out plant parts for several different kinds of specimens, mix up the pieces. Then try to recreate each specimen from the different plant parts.

🐦 Store the plant parts pieces in a large plastic container with a lid. The Plant Parts Puzzle bin can be placed in an appropriate outdoor learning area or in your Ecology Action Research Station.

(continued)

🐚 Each time you go to the Ecology Action Research Station, look for a new plant neighbor to add to your Plant Parts Puzzle! Also, record the plant of the day in your nature journal.

🐚 Look at a live plant in the meadow and try to answer the following questions:

- Which part of the plant helps it drink?
- Which part of the plant helps keep it in one place?
- Which part of the plant holds the plant upright?
- Which part of the plant holds the flower parts together?
- Which part of the plant is open? Why?
- Why does your nose get yellow when you sniff a flower?
- Which part of the plant attracts bees?
- Why do flowers have colors?
- Why do flowers have petals?
- Why do your hands get sticky when you break the stem to pick it?
- Why do flowers grow in the meadow?
- Why do we plant flowers?

You might enjoy returning to a budded plant to watch the magical dance of an opening flower.

"THE GIFT OF
THE MEDICINAL PLANTS"

Grandforest Tree tells a story about how the gift of medicinal plants was brought to the humans.

I am an old tree, and very wise. I have seen many things - both good and bad. The following legend about the Gift of the Medicinal Plants tells of both conflict and harmony.

Once, a long, long time ago, people did not live in one place as they do now. They wandered through vast forests and lush grasslands, hunting and gathering their food. It was a difficult way of life, for food was often scarce and the traveling exhausting . Back then, people did not live for very long, and no one knew how to heal the sick or injured.

Because of this, the human population was increasing very slowly. This concerned the Gods, Goddesses, and Great Spirits that had put the humans on the earth, for they feared that the humans might become extinct. They held a council to discuss the problem. In the middle of this meeting, they heard the sound of a child crying. When they looked to the source of this sorrowful noise, they discovered a young girl in a cave - cold, lonely, and very frightened. This gave them an idea.

One of the Goddesses disguised herself as a rabbit, and hopped into the dark, damp cave. She nuzzled the terrified child and, speaking softly asked, "What is wrong, my friend? Why are you crying?" And the little girl, whose name was Nayarta, told her story. She had been separated from her family during a violent thunderstorm that had taken her by surprise on the open grasslands. Rain had pelted her, lightning had flashed and the thunder had exploded in her ears, forcing her to seek shelter in the cave. She felt she was being punished for always lagging behind, looking at interesting plants and collecting flowers, or talking to trees and animals on the side of the trail.

The Goddess-as-rabbit snuggled up to Nayarta and soothed her fears. "Do not worry little one, I will keep you company. And I will ask my friends to join me, so you will never be alone."

Nayarta gathered wood for a fire and grass for a bed. She slept soundly next to a warm fire and the furry rabbit. That night she had a wonderful dream. In the dream she climbed into the inviting branches of an ancient gnarled Oak tree. The Oak tree welcomed her into its nest of sturdy branches and told Nayarta it had been waiting for her. "Nayarta, you are a gift to the humans on earth. Your fascination with plants will bring comfort and health to humankind. Your unique relationship with plants will allow you to learn from them, and they wish to share their healing knowledge with you. Listen carefully to what they have to say!"

The next morning Nayarta went to bathe in the little river that swept past the cave. On her way down the steep embankment she slipped and fell, cutting her knee and banging her head on a rock. She lay still for a few minutes, bleeding, her head pounding. Then she heard a voice next to her - it was Plantain talking. "Nayarta, Nayarta! Gather my leaves and crush them between two stones. Then place my mashed leaves over your cut. Cover the leaves with soft Moss and tie in place with a braid of Timothy."

Nayarta did just that. The cool Moss soothed the sting and absorbed the blood, and the Plantain soon stanched the bleeding. Her head however, still hurt. As she hobbled back towards the cave with her rabbit - friend, another voice called to her. It was Valerian. "Nayarta, I

can help relieve your headache. Dig my roots, pound them between stones and use the pounded roots to make a tea." Nayarta was pleasantly surprised when her head stopped throbbing after drinking the warm Valerian tea.

That was just the beginning of Nayarta's training. Again and again plants would call her attention to them and teach her their healing magic. As the years passed, she learned medicinal uses of many plants. She kept a medicine bag containing leaves, roots and bark with her all the time. Sometimes she would treat an injured animal, or herself when she was ill. In this way she became very knowledgeable and wise about the gifts of plants.

Many years later, Nayarta happened upon a group of people camped by the edge of a river. She instantly recognized the colorful designs and beadwork that decorated the people's clothing. She could tell by the shape of the crude shelters that the tribe was her own! She slowly walked to the edge of the camp, waiting for people to notice her. Soon a curious crowd gathered around her. Speaking hesitantly through hand signs - many of which Nayarta had forgotten - she introduced herself as Nayarta, daughter of Sohowi and Gabut. But many years had passed, and no one seemed to remember her. She had cured herself of many illnesses using the healing power of the plants. Because of this she had lived much longer than most humans. Sohowi and Gabut and her brothers and sisters had been dead many years. Only one grandson, Tetsin, was left. Himself an elder, Tetsin was now the leader of the tribe. Sadly, he had been ill for many moons and now lay on his deathbed.

The people were wary of Nayarta, for how could she have lived for so long in the wilderness by herself? Perhaps she was one of the Great Spirits in disguise! Then, an elderly blind woman who had been sightless since birth, touched Nayarta's face and recognized her. Nayarta asked to see her ailing nephew, the chief who lay

She pointed to her pouch and signaled that she might be able to help him.

Still a little fearful, but eager to help their leader, the people led Nayarta to Tetsin's bedside. She asked for hot water, and began mixing herbs from her pouch. Confident and directive, she asked some children to collect the soft velvet-like leaves that grew at the base of the Mullein plant. After mixing several different herbs and steeping them in hot water, she fed the tea to Tetsin. He drank and seemed to relax, then fell into a deep sleep. Nayarta stayed by his side, feeding him the tea each time he woke. After two days, Tetsin was able to sit up. He was walking soon after that, and within a week he was feeling better than he had in a long, long time.

And so Nayarta became the first "Medicine Woman." Childless and too old to bear children, she took on Kaya, Tetsin's bright and eager granddaughter, as an apprentice. In time Kaya became the tribe's next Medicine Woman. She, in turn, taught her daughter everything she knew, and so the knowledge was passed down through the ages.

That is how the use of medicinal plants came to humans. It all started, remember, with a little girl whose fascination with plants allowed her to listen, really listen, to what the plants had to say.

MEADOW MEDICINALS
FOR
HEALTH AND FIRST AID

If you familiarize yourself with nature lore, Nature's remedies and tonics are always close at hand.

When bee-sting or bite bring you a pain
Look to the Earth for Friend Plantain.
She lies low with ribbed full leaf
Chew it, dab it, for instant relief!
Plantain heals the pain

Common Plantain

This tried and true remedy may come in handy more than once during Spring. Learning to identify **plantain**, which grows in any lawn, will enable you to treat bee stings swiftly and with satisfaction. Gently "chew" the Plantain ribs. This releases the juices of the plant, which immediately soothes bee stings. After removing the stinger, gently dab the juices of Friend Plantain on the sting. Don't forget to say thanks to Friend Plantain!

Thank you Sister Clover Blossom
For your sunshine tastes so sweet.
When I walk through wildflower meadows
You are such a tasty treat!

Clover's large, purple blossoms begin to perfume the meadow just before Summer Solstice, June 23rd. For a quick pick-me-up after a hot day of meadow adventures, pluck the blossoms parts from the flower head. Suck on the white tips at the base of the flower parts and you'll know why bees love to feast on clover. Only purple clover heads are sweet. Pink or white clover heads are rather bland. Try the taste test yourself!

When Sun Spirit sends the sunbeams down
Each plants a kiss upon the ground.
And where their lips have touched the Earth
A tiny flower's given birth.
All are here with gifts to please
Of beauty, food, and cures for disease.

Wood sorrel

🌿 You can supplement **Spring's first salads** by foraging for delicacies on the school lawn. For an extra vitamin A boost, wash and add tender young **dandelion** greens to your salads. These Vitamin A foods are the "Glow Foods" that nourish your skin and hair.

Look, too, for **sourgrass**, which is also know as **oxalis** or **sorrel**. The leaves of this grass have a tart flavor that freshen the

breath. The leaves add Vitamin C to your diet, and give some zing to Nature's spring salad bar. All Vitamin C foods are part of the "Glow Food" Family.

Want To Do More?

• **Create a Meadow Medicinals and Edibles learning area at your EARS station.** Inside a large plastic bin covered with a lid, store wildflower identification necklaces for any medicinals and edibles you find growing in the meadow.

To make identification necklaces, you will need:
3 x 5 cards
clear Contact paper
Peterson's <u>Guide to Wildflowers</u>
container with lid

1) Use 3 x 5 index cards to laminate illustrations or dried pressed specimens of clover, plantain, dandelion, or oxalis.

2) Note any distinguishing characteristics of the plant, such as leaf patterns, stem type (woolly, spiked, smooth, reddish), petal or sepal patterns. Highlight these characteristics on the laminated illustration.

3) On the reverse side of the illustration card, record medicinal and edible uses of the plant. Punch a hole in the index card and string it with yarn so it can be worn around your neck as an identification tool when you are hiking in the meadow.

4) Put all the identification necklaces into a container with a lid to use as a first aid station. Place the container near an appropriate out-door learning area. Post a **wildflower first aid sign** or **banner** along-side the container. This banner could be a plant with a red cross, a band-aid overlay, or whatever you think will be eye-catching. Be sure to use indelible fabric paints or crayons on the banner. For the sign, use permanent marker or paint.

• Each time you go to the Meadow Medicinals container, choose a new identification card. Spend some time getting to know all your meadow neighbors.

✍ Don't forget to illustrate Meadow Medicinals in your **nature journal.** Record and the learn the poems in this activity so you can give a language arts recital.

THE SEED MAKERS

"When the flower blossoms, the bee comes uninvited."

What is the supportive relationship between insects and flowers in seed production? By looking carefully at a flower and the meadow insects that visit it, a delightful model can be made to represent how seeds are made.

You will need:

magnifying lenses
beeswax or plasticene
tissue paper
play dough
pipe cleaners
cornmeal or dyed yellow flour
drinking straws

🐝 On a Spring walk, sit down a short distance from some spring bulbs, apple blossoms, or wildflowers. Study the **different parts that make up a flower blossom.** See if you can locate five separate flower sections.

- Do you see brightly-colored **petals** cupped together?
- Are there green, dish-like **sepals** below the petals, holding them in place?
- Can you find a **stamen** and **pistil** in the flower's center?
- Does **golden pollen** cover some of the pistil and stamen? Pollen is a golden powder that sometimes rubs off on your nose when you sniff a flower. It's fun to look at a friend whose nose is covered with pollen!

🐝 If you sit quietly a few feet from the flower, you might have the good fortune to **observe the different insects that visit flowers.** Watch what they do.

- Does every insect visitor do the same thing?

● What are insects looking for in flowers?
● What do they take away with them?

❧ Look on the insect's body for **golden pollen powder**. Do you see how the insect carries the pollen from one part of the flower and rubs it onto another? The father part - the **stamen** - makes the pollen. The mother part - the **pistil** - usually receives a dusting of pollen when the insect is foraging for food. Once the mother part is dusted with pollen, it makes seeds so the flower family can continue.

❧ While sitting near the flower, **create a model** of its blossom as well as a drawing of the insects that visit it. If you can't work near a live specimen, perhaps you can bring a flower bouquet indoors for study. Flower models can be made from beeswax or plasticene. You can also use tissue paper to make petals, play dough to make sepals, and create stamen from pipe cleaners. Dust the stamen with cornmeal pollen or flour dyed yellow with tumeric or curry powder. Use wrapped tissue paper to make pistils.

❧ How would you make a model of a pollinating insect? Attach a model insect to the end of a pipe cleaner, then try pollinating your model flower!

❧ If you visit your flower next Fall, initiate a **seed search** to see if the pollinators have done their important work!

Remember, insects fertilize flowers as they gather nectar. The pollen from the male stamen is carried by insects during their nectar-gathering process and rubbed onto the female pistil. This **fertilization process** allows seeds to form.

❧ The next generation's seeds are usually cradled around the mother and father parts of the flower. Can you find them?
How would you describe the ways in which flowers and insects cooperate? How do you feel about insects?

To Be An Ant

Today you are going to pass through an incredible shrinking machine, which will turn you into the size of an ant.

R eady? Crawl through the arms of two people hold
ing hands. While still crawling, close your eyes.
Pretend you are as tiny as an ant. Do you feel
yourself shrinking?

You are in a meadow - everything around you is
huge! As you creep about, looking for something to eat,
your ant eyes notice many details: a grain of sand is almost as large as a stone, blades of grass are very green
when seen so near, a drop of dew is as big as you. And
listen! Feel the earth rumble as something <u>very large</u>
passes by. It must be a human. Oooo, the sound of its
footsteps hurts your little ant ears. But, phew! The human
keeps on going. You're safe.

As soon as your heartbeat returns to normal, you
decide to explore a dandelion. Wow, it's as tall as a tree!
Its blossoms spread all about you, a dazzling yellow field.
As you crawl across this brilliant yellow meadow, you feel
the softness of its petals beneath your feet. Ahh, smell the
fresh dandelion scent.

Now you scurry down the trunk of the dandelion tree
and begin to march through a jungle of grass. Each blade
towers above your head, like a sinuous green skyscraper
reaching for the blue, blue sky. You wonder what it would
be like to climb to the top of one of these blades of grass -
what might you see from such a high place? You choose a
stem that seems to tower above all the others. Gingerly,
you begin creeping up the fragile stem, not knowing

whether it will hold your weight. It does! Your confidence soars as you climb up, up, up. After a few seconds of climbing, you find yourself high above all the other blades of grass. What a view! You are surrounded by a sea of grass waving in the soft summer winds. Splotches of brilliant colors contrast with the soft, green sea - more tree flowers to explore!

Suddenly, the stem you are clinging to is stirred by a

brisk breeze. Hold on tight! The grass sways in a long gentle sweep, like an ocean wave - what a ride! Up and down, back and forth, swishing, swirling in the wind. As abruptly as it begins, the breeze dies down. Gradually, the blade of grass ceases to move. What fun! But you've had enough adventures for one day, so you quickly climb down the stem before the next breeze comes along, and begin to make your way towards a huge daisy you spied from the grass tower.

On your way to the daisy you meet another ant. Using your antennae, which pick up chemical messages and translate them into a meaningful language, you check to see if this ant is from your village. The ant you've met is equally curious about you, and touches your antennae with his. You detect a familiar scent - which means this ant shares a home with you. He has been out looking for food, and has found chocolate cake crumbs left over from a human picnic! But you are on a quest, and decide to continue your adventure.

As you leave your fellow ant, however, you are tempted by the chemical trail he lays down to show others where the food is located. Hmmm. . . should you go snack on some chocolate cake, or hike up a Daisy Tree? Only you can decide. What does your ant body most want to do?

🐜 Once the shrinking machine experience is over, don't forget to return to your normal size. Tell others about the amazing things you learned through an ant's eyes! How did you feel being shrunk to the size of an ant? Does size have any relationship to the value you add to the world? Your answers to these questions may inspire follow-up inquiries.

You might want to leave a permanent shrinking machine close by with instructions for its use. Use your imagination to do this!

✎ Also, you might like to **illustrate a short story** about your experiences.

Ant Math, Nature's Way

- How many ants do you think live in an ant village?
- How many legs do these ants have altogether?
- If an ant described you to another ant, how many times taller would it say you were?
- Ants and the number six seem to go together. Can you add or multiply by sixes?

THROUGH THE EYES OF AN ANT

What do ants do? To find out, follow an ant as it comes and goes!

🐜 **Look around the meadow for ant activity**. Gather around an anthill and observe the life of an ant colony. Answer as many of the following questions as you can, then look to the ants for the other answers.

- What does an ant look like? Describe and illustrate its body parts.
- What tasks does each part of an ant's body perform?
- Do all ants look the same?
- What different tasks do you see ants performing?
- How do ants interact with each other?
- Do any of the ants cooperate with others? How?
- Where are the ants going?
- What does an anthill look like?
- How many ants did you observe in the ant village?
- What is the role of the ant in the Nature Neighborhood?

🐜 If business seems slow around an anthill, here's a way to coax them into action. Spread some crumbs a foot or two below the anthill. Now sit tight and watch the amazing display of the ant world!

🐜 **What happens when the ants emerge from their shelter?** The ants you see outside the nest are usually wingless worker ants. Acting cooperatively, they take care of household tasks for the entire ant colony. Worker ants have several ways of organizing the others to gather food crumbs. How many ways do you see?

Did you notice any ants riding piggyback to the food crumbs? Or did each ant simply go about its own business, not stopping to communicate with the others in any way? Well, the ants are not ignoring one another. Ants live in dark, earthen burrows, but although they have little need for sight their sense of smell is highly developed. As they go about the business of collecting the crumbs, they lay down a scented trail from the food to the hill. For this reason, they don't always need to stop, chat and give directions to one another.

🐜 **Try this experiment.** Gently rub away the odor in the area where the trail seems to be established. Do you see any confused behavior among the ants as they try to return to their burrows without the aid of a scented trail? What do the ants do to find their way back?

Here's another way ants communicate a food source to one another. An ant returning from the food source may use its antennae to smell another ant and determine whether it belongs to the same nest. The ant's powerful antennae can help her identify sisters who are descendants of the same Queen. To lead her sister ant back to the food, the lead ant rubs her sister's antennae as they return to the food source. Aren't ant neighbors amazing?

✍ **Record your ant eye observations in your nature journal.** Can you draw a map of the ant people's village you visited? Include the anthill, or the path the ant took to get from place to place.

Near the ant village, mark the anthill with a sign saying **"Ant Village, Walk with Care"**. Draw a map of the ant village and post it nearby. In a large plastic container with a lid, store illustrations of different ants and list their roles in the ant colony. Visitors to the ant village can look for each of these fantastic social nature neighbors. The visitors must use their own ant eyes to do so of course!

ANT NEIGHBORHOODS: BUILDING AN ANT FARM

Ants live in families, with thousands of relatives, in underground nests that very much resemble a village setting. What do you think their village looks like? Build an Ant Farm and find out!

How can it be possible that all the ants in a village are related? A queen resides in every ant village. She is the mother of all the ants in that colony. But it is unlikely that your Ant Farm will have a queen ant, for queens are very rare and hard to find!

> ☞ *Note: A month ago you should have sent away for ant materials and the ant coupon, which now must be returned to the company for the delivery of the live ants you will be studying on your Ant Farm. It will take 2-3 weeks before the ants arrive. In the meantime, if you haven't ordered a preconstructed Ant Farm from the company, build a home to welcome your new friends!*

You will need:

two 2" x 4"'s, each of them eight inches long
one 2" x 4", nineteen inches long
nails
two 9" x 18" plexiglass sheets
a drill
thirty 1" rubber squares
thirty 1" screws
sheer fabric to cover the top of the Ant Farm
tacks
a small sponge
a piece of dark felt, cloth or paper to cover the sides of the Ant Farm

Construction steps:

1) To make the frame: Lay the nineteen-inch 2" x 4" board on its 2" side. On top of this piece, one at each end in an upright position, place the two, eight-inch 2" x 4" boards. Nail or screw the eight-inch pieces to the nineteen-inch piece.

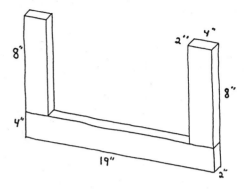

2) Attach the two 9" x 18" plexiglass pieces to the front and back of the frame by carefully drilling holes through the plexiglass and into the wood (the top of the the plexiglass should be even with the top of the frame). Drill four holes on each side, and seven on the bottom.

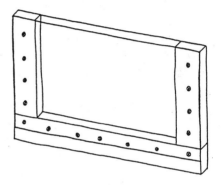

3) Drill a hole in the center of each of the rubber squares (these will cover the holes to protect the plexiglass from the metal screws).

4) With the rubber squares in place, screw the plexiglass to the frame. Make sure the plexiglass is flush against the wood to prevent the ants from escaping.

5) Fill the Ant Farm with sand, leaving a 1-1/2" space at the top.

6) To make a cover for the top of the Ant Farm, cut a length of sheer fabric that is escape-proof but which will permit good air circulation. Double layers of screening work well. Tack or staple the fabric to the top of the Ant Farm, leaving a small opening.

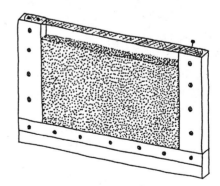

7) This hole gives you controlled access to the ants. You can water and feed them through the hole by inserting into it a moist sponge and food scraps. Close it by securing the fabric against the wood with tacks. Be sure the hole is closed tightly, or the ants will escape!

8) Ants live underground, where it is quite dark, so the next step is to make a wrapper for the sides of the Ant Farm. Black felt, dark cloth or dark paper work fine. If you wish, decorate the wrapper. For example, everyone can contribute an ant made of fabric or felt, which can be attached to the wrapper. Or the class may wish to draw an Ant Farm scene on the wrapper. Remember to keep the sides of the Ant Farm covered until you want to peek inside - ants like their privacy!

❧ When the ants arrive, shout "Hooray!"

♥ Count the ants as you carefully place them into the farm through the opening. This can be done by gently removing them one at a time with the bristles of a watercolor paintbrush. But you'll have to work quickly to keep the ants you placed inside from climbing out!

♥ After the ants are safely nestled in their new home, place a small, wet sponge on top of the sand, along with any one of the following:

> some sugar crystals
> bread or cracker crumbs
> grass seeds
> food provided by the ant supplier.

♥ Find a place for your Ant Farm away from direct sun and heat.

♥ To prevent ants from escaping, surround the Ant Farm with a moat. You can do this by putting the Ant Farm in a 1/2" deep pan and then adding a little water to the pan. Make sure the water level does not rise above the wooden base of the Ant Farm. Otherwise you might flood the ants' home!

♥ It's fun to mount a stationary magnifying lens in front of the Ant Farm to observe the finer details of ant anatomy and communication.

✍ Watch what an ant family does! You might want to record and illustrate your observations in your **ant journal**.

A DAY IN THE LIFE OF AN ANT: AN ANT WATCH

Have you ever wondered what the ants visiting your picnic blanket were doing before you arrived? How does this clean-up crew know you are there? What do they do in their village beneath the soil? You can discover the answers to some of these mysteries when you go on an ant watch!

If you spend time studying the Ant Farm, you will discover things you never imagined!

🐜 First (but only if you feel comfortable doing so), remove an ant from the Ant Farm with a watercolor brush and place it in your hand. Watch closely. What do you notice about your new friend? How does it feel when the little critter moves about on your hand? After a few minutes, gently put the ant back in its home.

🐜 Look at the ants busily crawling around in the Ant Farm. Can you find one ant that looks different from all the others? What does this ant look like? Observe every special part of this ant. Can you draw what you see in your journal?

🐜 Observe this ant for several minutes.

- Where does it go?
- What happens when it meets another ant?
- Can you imitate the movements of this ant on its daily journey?
- Can you write a story, song or poem about it in your journal?
- What name would you give to this ant to describe the qualities you've observed?

🐜 Write down all the questions you would like to ask this ant.

🐜 Here are some things to think about:

- Ants are very special creatures. What characteristics do they have that make them special?
- Do you and ants share any of the same needs?
- Is there anything you discovered about this ant that could help you in your own life? How are you and this ant alike?
- How could you design an ant costume? If you want to see what it feels like to be an ant for a day, wear the costume for the Spring Fling.

🐜 You might want to maintain an **ant watch** for several days, or keep watch once a week for an entire month. Keep track of the questions you noted in your journal, and see whether all of them get answered during these ant watches.

✍ Try any of the following creative writing topics:

- If you could let everyone in the world know about your discoveries of the mysteries of the ant world, what would you want them to know?
- One day, you meet an Ant Person strolling down the road. The two of you make friends. Write about the things you do together.
- Rewrite the words to the song "The Ants Come Marching One by One, Hurrah! Hurrah!" Sing this song to an ant lover.
- Write a story from the perspective of an ant.

Want To Do More?

In the company of a small group of friends, take turns telling creative stories about ants. For an additional challenge, have a friend recall a story that was told the previous day. What does this tell you about the ability of people to communicate? How well do they listen?

ANT FAMILIES

What kinds of ants live in a colony? Are they all members of the same family? What role does each ant play in the colony? Observe the ant family in your Ant Farm during the next month, and see what you can learn!

🐜 **Do all ants in a family look or behave the same?** You might notice that some ants have wings and some do not. Newly-hatched queens and male ants have wings. Worker ants are not winged, and all workers are females.

🐜 **Why do males and new queens need to fly?** Since there is only one mature queen ant to a colony, newly-hatched young queen ants swarm from the colony when warm weather arrives, looking for a place to start their own colonies. Winged male ants mate with the new queens, then they die. Queens try to find a new colony of their own, but not all succeed. What happens to the ones who don't? Could it be that they are eaten, or killed by the wind or a storm?

🐜 **Do ants exist that don't resemble ants?** Tiny eggs, each the size of a pinpoint, hatch into larvae. The larvae are about 1/4 inch long and resemble grains of rice. They are fed by worker or nurse ants, who care for the young ants in the nursery. Watch closely and you might see the larvae eating and being cared for by the worker or nurse ants. Some of the larvae are fed a special food so they will become queen ants. See if this happens in your nursery.

🐜 **Is there a nursery in your Ant Farm?** Pay close attention to the various tasks the nurse ants perform as they care for the young that are hatching. Although nurse ants never have babies of their own, they seem to care for the queen's babies is if they were mothers themselves.

↜ **What are some of the other tasks the nurses perform?** The oval, mummy-like cases you see are actually pupae, which have been spun by the larvae. You may notice a nurse ant holding up a pupa as it breaks from its mummy case, and another nurse ant feeding the newly-emerged baby before it fully leaves its shell. Nurse ants feed young ants directly from their own mouths, regurgitating food until baby ants are old enough to feed themselves. You may see nurse ants cleaning emerging ants and straightening out their crumpled legs.

↜ **What color are newly-emerging ants?** Are they lighter than the adult ants?

↜ **Why do nurse ants seem so very busy?** Actually, they are determined to keep the nursery in order. You might notice the nurse ants arranging the babies according to size. Some people believe the nurses are trying to be prepared in case there is an attack on the ant nest. The nurses will save the more fully grown young larvae and carry them from the nest to a safe location.

↜ Ants keep their nests very clean. See if you can discover where they pile their refuse.

↜ **Can you find a graveyard in your ant farm?** Ants will often bury their dead sisters and brothers in a mass grave.

(continued)

Want To Do More?

   In your journal, write about and draw all the daily activities you observe ants doing. Draw ants that seek food and feed others. Can you draw a nurse ant taking care of a baby? Draw a group of ants cleaning house. Try drawing all the stages of the life of an ant.

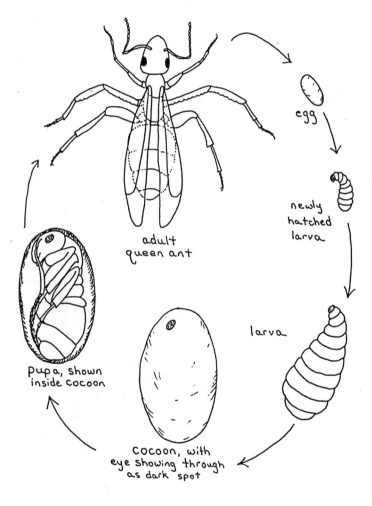

adult
queen ant

egg

newly
hatched
larva

larva

pupa, shown
inside cocoon

cocoon, with
eye showing through
as dark spot

   Feel free to use the "Stages of An Ant" graphic as a guide or model for drawing a large, colored chalk illustration on the blackboard.

Ant Trivia ❧

- What do you see ants doing?
- What jobs do different ants have?
- Do ants ever sleep?
- How does each ant change and grow?
- How do ants communicate?
- How might you compare the stages of an ant's life to your own?
- How are all the ants in a colony related?
- Can you compare the roles of different ants in ant families to human family roles?
- Which ant role would you like to pursue in an ant family?
- Are ants important in your neighborhood? Why?

Ant Math, Nature's Way

❧ How many ants are in your Ant Farm neighborhood?

❧ If an ant can lift five times its weight, how much could you lift if you were an ant?

❧ If an ant can lift five times its weight, how many ants would it take to lift you?

❧ Can you count by sixes, doing an ant dance with a partner?

The Counting Ant Dance

1) Stand facing your partner. Count **six** as you pat your hands on top of your head.

2) Count to **twelve** as you put both your hands on your shoulders.

3) Count to **eighteen** as you clap your hands.

4) Count to **twenty-four** as you and your partner clap one another's hands.

5) Place your hands on your hips and count to **thirty**.

6) Count to **thirty-six,** slapping your knees.

7) Can you guess what comes next? Add six to thirty-six, and you get **forty-two!** Lift your right foot behind your back and count to forty-two as you slap your sole.

(continued)

8) Finally, count to **forty-eight**, this time slapping your left sole. Now proceed in reverse, counting and performing the accompanying numerical patterns "forty-eight, forty-two, thirty-six, thirty, twenty-four, eighteen, twelve, six". Whew, have you got the rhythm and coordination of a six-legged ant?

QUEEN OF THE HILL

There is only one Ant Queen in the village and she is mother to them all! What is an Ant Queen like?

🐜 If you can find and observe the Queen Ant, you will notice she is .different from the other ants in the colony. She gets a lot of attention. Where does she reside in the ant hill? The Queen has her own royal quarters where she is surrounded by worker sisters who busily lick her clean and feed her royal food. The Queen Ant spends a lot of time eating or being groomed. What duties does the Queen Ant perform? Continuation of the colony is her only task as she lays eggs the size of a pin point.

🐜 Did you discover that all ants in one village are related because the Queen is the only egg layer? How do all the other relatives care for her and her colony?

🐜 Do you and ants need any of the same things in order to have a full life?

AN ANT FOOD EXPERIMENT

Is there a food you could bring on a picnic that the ants wouldn't like? How can you find out which foods ants prefer to eat? Design a research experiment to find out!

> Find a friend who likes experiments and plan one together.

1) Write down what it is you are trying to prove.

2) Decide how you will go about doing the experiment. For ex ample, are you trying to learn whether certain foods attract ants?
Are you trying to discover whether certain foods or herbs repel ants?

3) What actions will protect the health and safety of the ants during the experiment? What might endanger them? Decide what experiments you feel comfortable about.

4) Record each step, and the events that occur as you perform the step.

> What do you think you learned? Share your findings with others.

Remember, research means looking for something over and over again until you find it. What would you like to do again? What more do you wish you knew?

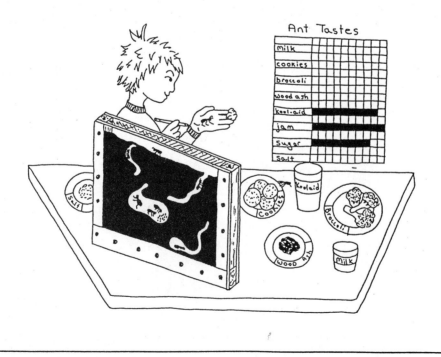

THE ANTS COME MARCHING ONE BY ONE, HURRAH, HURRAH!

By now you've probably discovered that every ant is interesting and special. You can celebrate this good news by sharing your findings in a culminating presentation.

🐜 **Invite** the rest of the school, your parents and community members. The presentation might include:

- **Artwork** depicting ants.

- **Displays** of ant colonies.

- **Charts** describing ant metamorphosis.

- **Reports** to parent and community members about the importance of ants in the environment.

🐜 **A brochure** of interesting facts about the types of food ants like and don't like, as well as how, with care, to avoid ants in your home.

🐜 **A play about the Queen Ant and her royal family.** Ant costumes for ant family members are easy to make - and fun!

- Dress like an ant, wearing black pants and a black, long sleeve shirt. Attach a set of **antennae** to the crown of your head.

- Your chest can be the **thorax**. If you have observed an ant closely, you know that its **legs** are attached to its thorax. Your own legs and arms make up two pairs of legs. The third pair can be made of cardboard, jointed with brass clip fasteners so they really move!

so it hangs between your legs.

● The nurse ants can wear Red Cross arm bands. Male ants wear wings. The big Queen sports a crown and wings, and is fed from a jelly jar all day.

Hurrah for ants!

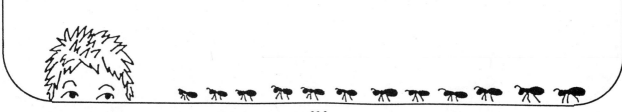

BIRD WATCHER'S PARAPHERNALIA

In the Spring, keep watch at the bird feeder and you will be able to observe and record the different species of returning birds. What is different about each species of birds?

Learn to identify the many species and observe their winter habits. To prepare for this activity, make various bird watching charts, graphs and I.D. cards for documenting your feathered friends.

You will need:

a burlap pouch (see *Winter* "Birds of a Feather
    I.D. Center", page 137)
<u>Golden Guide to Birds</u>

(continued)

plastic containers
a variety of birdseed, such as sunflower seed,
    thistle, or cracked corn

🐦 **Hang a bird identification pouch** near the bird feeding window to keep track of who's who at the feeder.

Keep your bird I.D. cards handy in a sewn burlap or fabric pouch that contains several pockets. Bird cards can be made from laminated _Golden Guide_ pictures. Simply cut out a page and cover it with clear Contact paper. Since both sides of a page have bird illustrations, you will need to decide whether you want single- or double-sided cards. Laminate the illustrations onto cardboard accordingly. When a bird appears at the feeder, find the appropriate card and place it in a pocket of your bird identification pouch.

🐦 **Chart your daily sightings** on a tally sheet and keep it in the identification pouch. Which are the most commonly attracted birds to the feeders? The least? The most colorful? The most greedy? Largest? Smallest? In which season or month does each bird visit?

🐦 **Observe and record birds** that frequent your feeder. **Identify the various parts** of each bird, including wing bar design, crown, eye ring, throat, beak design, breast, tail feathers, rump, feet. See the "Beauty of Birds" activity graphics on page 139 to refresh your memory.

🐦 **Can you identify the male and female** of each species? Do the special markings of individual birds serve a particular purpose? Unique characteristics that aid animals are called **adaptations**. How might adaptations help birds? Choose a particular bird, then draw the male and female markings of that species. Why do males and females of the same species have different markings?

🐦 On a daily basis, **observe and record bird seed choices** at the feeding station. Which birds prefer which seeds?

> ✿ Set out plastic containers, each containing a different kind of seed - such as cracked corn, sunflower, thistle. Be sure to measure the bird seed carefully before putting it out, other-

wise you won't get an accurate reading of the amount of food eaten. A suggested measurement is one cupful of each kind of seed.

- How much bird seed is eaten each day?
- Graph the number of cupfuls birds eat each week or month. This will help you estimate the amount of bird feed required for a season.

❧ What type of beak serves what kind of eating function?
Draw a bird, paying special attention to its beak and the type of bird feed it prefers.

❧ Observe birds in the Nature Neighborhood as they raise their young during the Spring. After several days of observation, you should be able to identify new families.

- What kind of shelter does the bird use for its nesting site?
- When male and female birds raise their young, does each perform a different job? Or the same job?
- How does a bird's spring plumage differ from its winter plumage?

A DAY IN THE LIFE OF A BIRD

What can you learn from observing a bird for a day? Watch, and see!

Observe a single bird in your nature neighborhood for an entire day, monitoring its movements as it busily goes about its work. Observe the bird's feeding area, its singing perches, and its general territory. Watch it as it travels to gather food, defends its territory, takes a bird bath, preens its feathers, gets some exercise in flight, and does all the things birds do in their daily lives.

Urban birders don't have to travel far to observe birds in action. Pigeons and sparrows nest and shelter under eaves, between the letters of neon signs, on statue heads, and in other interesting places. Sponsor a contest with your friends to see who can discover the most unusual location of a nesting bird!

🐦 Document some of these interesting details in your nature journal. Here are a few ideas:

- Write down any questions you have regarding what the bird does during the day.
- Observe the bird in flight. What does it look like? How does it use or flap its wings when flying? How and where does it land?
- What kind of behavior does the bird exhibit when defending its territory? Does a pair of birds guard the nest or feed the young? How do they act? How do they communicate with each other?
- What kind of food does the bird forage for? How far does it go and where does it go to do its searching? How much time each day is spent gathering and eating food?
- What special adaptation does the bird have for camouflage? For flying? Protection? Communication? Gathering food?
- What habitats does the bird prefer for nesting sites? For food gathering? For its territory?
- Make a map of the area where the bird lives. Include the nesting tree site, how far the bird flies to get food, and how much territory the bird "defends".

🐦 Set up a **Nesting Bird Watch Area**. This can be near your EARS station or at another convenient location. If working with a group, divide into pairs to conduct ten minute shifts for observing and documenting birds. When all shifts are complete, share the data. Post a sign reading *"Hush! Birds Nesting"* in the area of the nesting birds. Invite others in small, quiet groups to visit the site. Make a laminated map of the nesting bird's territory and show it to those who can't go to the site. Challenge the group with a checklist, asking them to locate singing perches, food sites, types of food foraged, and to identify body parts of the bird.

BIRD LIFE NOTE CARDS

Make and sell these beautiful Bird Life Note Cards to earn money for the purchase of birdhouse materials.

You can make these simple cards, which resemble stained glass, by following these instructions.

You will need:

an assortment of colored tissue paper scraps
white glue
scissors
recycled yogurt containers of water (for mixing glue solutions)
Q-tips or small paint brushes
waxed paper
strong paper for greeting cards
envelopes to fit cards
bird-shaped templates cut from sturdy paper or cardboard

Directions to make stained glass Bird Life Note Cards:

1) In recycled yogurt containers, dilute some white glue with water. Stir the mixture with a paintbrush or Q-tip until the solution is runny.

2) Tear large squares of waxed paper and lay them down in the work area.

3) Make a collage of torn pieces of colored tissue paper, laying them out on top of the wax paper.

4) Apply the glue-water solution to the tissue paper scraps, piecing them together to form a large piece of multi-colored tissue paper that resembles stained glass.

5) Allow the glued-together tissue paper to dry completely as it lies on the waxed paper. (This may take overnight, depending upon moisture levels.)

6) Gently remove the dried, stained glass tissue paper from the waxed paper.

7) Here are two options for designing your cards:

Option #1
• Using a bird template, trace the outline of a bird on a postcard-size card.
• Cut the outline from the card.
• Using strong tape, attach a square or rectangular piece of stained glass tissue paper to the inside of the card over the cut-out.
• Write greetings on the reverse side (the front) of the card.
• Display the card in a window so that light shines through it.

Option #2
• Using a bird template, trace the outline of a bird on a piece of stained glass tissue paper.
• Cut out the bird, then paste it with full-strength, white glue onto heavy stock, greeting card paper.
• Press the cutout beneath a heavy book until the glue dries.
• Write the name of the bird on the card.

Interesting facts about the bird can be noted on the backs of both cards.

Raise funds for bird projects in your community by selling Bird Life Note Cards in packages of six. (Include envelopes for the cards!)

NEIGHBORHOOD BIRD PROJECT

Have you ever noticed how people in a park love to get close to pigeons? This city experience proves that it's not necessary to trek into the forest to watch birds. Design and build a bird watching area in your neighborhood, complete with a bird blind, birdhouses or feeders, and a place to sit and watch. Now invite friends or community elders to enjoy the fine art of bird watching!

🐦 Do the members of your community have a favorite place where they like to walk and gather quietly in nice weather? Would this place be a likely location for a bird feeding station, nesting boxes, birdhouses, or a bird blind? Look for a protected area, where bushes or trees provide some natural cover. Once you've found a place, it's time to plan and implement the project.

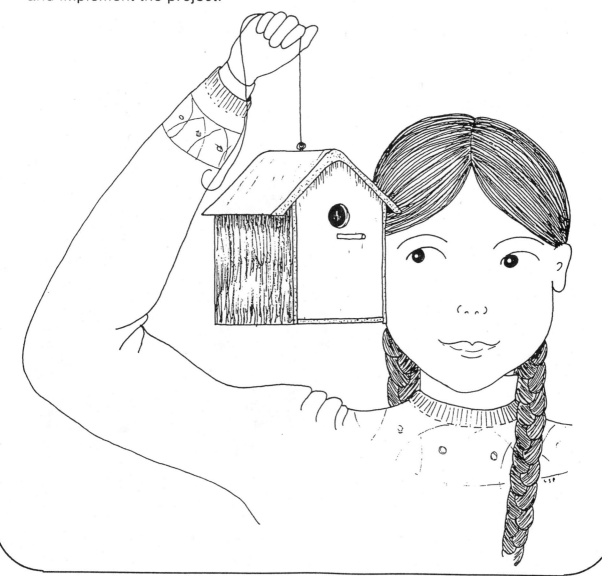

🐦 **Research birdhouse and feeder designs** so you can build the proper structures for the birds that live in your area. (Bluebird houses may attract colonies of nearly extinct bluebirds to the area.) Next, obtain the materials you need and begin building!

🐦 **The design should be of a permanent nature,** so choose the proper materials and decide on the best construction technique. Walter Schutz's <u>How to Attract, House and Feed Birds</u> is a good how-to reference for designing and constructing birdhouses and feeders. Or design your own!

You will need:

wood
a saw
a measuring tape
a hammer
nails
waterproof paint or stain
hardware for hanging the birdhouses or feeders

1) Measure and cut wood.
2) Hammer or screw the pieces together.
3) If you paint the roof with a waterproof stain, the grain of the wood will remain visible.
4) Finish with a wood sealer <u>on the outside only</u> as wood sealer is toxic to birds!
5) Use appropriate hardware for hanging the feeder or birdhouse.

🐦 Once the birdhouses or feeders are finished, design a bird blind so you can observe the birds from a distance. You can even set up a park bench nearby. Then sit down, relax and enjoy the birds!

A SPRING FLING
IN THE
MEADOW-THICKET

Celebrate your meadow-thicket journey by sharing what you have learned with others!

Some suggestions for a Spring Fling Celebration follow. Elaborate on these suggestions - exercise your imagination, research ideas from your favorite activities. Make this a memorable community event!

A Spring Fling Celebration

🐌 **Create a Nature Neighborhood theater presentation**, complete with masks, a skit and dialogue representing voices of the Nature Neighborhood.

🐌 Write a play introducing the different **members of the meadow-thicket**. Present the play during the Spring Fling Celebration.

🐌 Demonstrate a **Web of Life** in the meadow-thicket. Have extra identification cards on hand, and invite fellow celebrants to participate.

🐌 Unveil your plans for a **Butterfly Garden**, and ask others to join you in planting it.

🐌 The morning of the Spring Fling Celebration, conduct a **spring bird count** in your neighborhood.

🐌 As an accompaniment to birdhouses or bird blind projects, **produce** a class journal of **spring bird identifications**. Distribute the journal at the Spring Fling Celebration, or give it as a gift to elders. Put a copy in the library for future reference.

On a hike, identify **Meadow Medicinal Plants** and explain their uses. Perhaps you can convince someone who knows a lot about these plants to come along and share what she knows.

On a walk, **identify all the different plants** you have discovered in your Nature Neighborhood.

Create a skit about the amazing world of ants.

Invite parents and community elders to help you construct birdhouses and feeders. Donate the houses or feeders to community elders, help them mount these wonderful gifts at their homes.

Explain to your guests why the days are growing longer - and warmer too!

Along with the bird food, butterfly food, and ant food, be sure to have some *people* food prepared as well!

Happy Spring!

Bibliography

Brody, Goldspinner, Green, Leventhal, Pocino. *Spinning Tales, Weaving Hope: Stories of Peace, Justice and the Environment,* New Society Publishers, PA, 1992.

Baylor, Byrd. *Hawk I'm Your Brother,* Alladin Books, NY, 1986.

Comstock, Anne B. *Handbook of Nature Study,* Cornell University Press, NY, 1974.

Cornell, Joseph. *Sharing the Joys of Nature: Nature Activities for All Ages,* Dawn Publications, CA,1989.

Damrosch, Barbara. *Theme Gardens,* Workman Publishing, 1982.

Deunsing, Edward. *Talking To Fireflies, Shrinking the Moon: A Parent's Guide and Nature Activities,* Plume Books, NY, 1990.

Facklam, Margery. *Do Not Disturb: The Mysteries of Animal Hibernation and Sleep,* Sierra Club, CA, 1989.

Harrison, George. *The Backyard Bird Watcher,* Simon & Schuster, NY, 1979.

Harrison, Kit and George. *The Birds of Winter,* Random House, NY, 1990.

Headstrom, Richard. *Adventures with Insects,* Dover Publications, NY, 1982.

Herman, Marina. *Teaching Kids to Love the Earth: Sharing A Sense of Wonder 186 Outdoor Activities for Parents and Other Teachers,* Pfeifer-Hamilton, CA, 1991.

Hunken, Jorie. *Bird Watching For All Ages, Activities for Children and Adults,* Globe Pequot Press, CT, 1992.

Martin, Alexander. *Golden Guide to Weeds,* Golden Press, NY, 1987.

Merilees, Bill. *Attracting Backyard Wildlife: A Guide for Nature Lovers,* Voyageur Press, Minnesota, 1989.

O'Toole, Christopher. *Discovering Ants,* Bookwright Press, NY, 1986.

Peterson, Lee. *A Field Guide to Edible Wild Plants,* Houghton Mifflin, Boston, 1977.

Schutz, Walter E. *How To Attract, House and Feed Birds,* Collier Books, NY, 1970.

Schwartz, David M. *The Hidden Life of the Meadow,* Crown Publishing, NY, 1988.

Stokes, Donald W. *A Guide to Nature in Winter,* Little, Brown and Company, Boston,1976.

Suzuki, David. *Looking at Insects,* Warner Books, NY, 1986.

Zim, Herbert. *Golden Nature Guide to Birds,* Golden Press, NY, 1956.

Zim, Herbert. *Golden Nature Guide to Flowers,* Golden Press, NY, 1950.

Recommended Children's Literature

Aesop's Fables has been published in many collections. These short stories are often told through the perspective of animals and provide food for thought in understanding our relationships with one another. Some suggested shorts include The North Wind and The Sun, Grasshopper and the Ants, and The House Mouse and the Field Mouse.

Aliki, ***A Weed Is a Flower: The Life of George Washington Carver,*** Simon and Schuster, NY, 1965. In this story we meet a special child who loved the natural world and grew up to become a man of the history books who contributed his understanding to the world. The idea that there may be a budding scientist inside every one of us is a good esteem builder, especially for children of color.

Arnosky, Jim, ***Crinklefoot's Book of Animal Tracking***, Bradbury Press, NY, 1979. Accompany Crinklefoot on his journey to discover how a beaver, racoon, deer, rabbit, bobcat and fox make tracks.

Arnosky, Jim, ***Secrets of a Wildlife Watcher,*** Lothrup Lee & Shepard, NY, 1983. Great tips for the amateur nature lover who wants to know how to spot wildlife signs. Wonderful sketches accompany the text.

Baylor, Byrd, ***Hawk I'm Your Brother***, Alladin Books, NY, 1986. A young boy who captures a hawk learns what it really means to fly.

Berger, Barbara, ***Gwinna,*** Philomel Books, NY, 1990. This read- aloud chapter book tells the story of no ordinary young child, Gwinna, who is sent to a childless couple by the Mother of the Owls. As she grows up Gwinna plays with the birds and sprouts real wings of her own, much to her parent's dismay. At her twelfth birthday, Gwinna must return to the Mother of the Owls. This enchanting tale tells of a girl who wants to use her own wings and sing her own song.

Bodecker, N.M., ***The Mushroom Center Disaster,*** Atheneum, NY, 1974. The small inhabitants of a meadow find their homes litterred by careless picknickers. They are very creative in discovering ways to make use of the dumped litter and reclaim their environment.

Cooney, Barbara, ***Miss Rumphius,*** Viking Press, NY, 1982. Miss Rumphius travels all over the world and retires to her home by the sea. Remembering a challenge by her grandfather when she was a young woman, she decides to leave something behind for the world and sets off to accomplish a wonderful task..... sowing wild flowers wherever she goes.

DePaola, Tomie, ***Legend of Bluebonnet,*** Putnam, 1983. A Native girl gives up her most treasured possession to save her people. In recognition for her full heart and self-sacrifice, the land is renewed.

Esbenson, Barbara, ***Ladder to the Sky,*** Little, Brown & Co., Boston, 1989. This Native legend tells of the time when the first healing herbs were given to humanity.

Gilchrist, Garth, ***Flying with the Swans*** (Cassette), Dawn Publications, Nevada City, CA. 95959 Guided visualizations take you through the life of a squirrel, butterfly, migrating goose, whale and tree.

Gryski, Camilla, ***Cat's Cradle, Owl's Eyes: A Book of String Games***, William Morrow & Co., NY, NY 1984

Hartman, Gail, ***As the Crow Flies: A First Book of Maps***, Bradbury Press, NY, 1991. This story shows the territory of several animals and then shows you how they see it through their own eyes. There's the Eagle's map, the Rabbit's map, the Crow's, the Horse's, the Seagull's and even the Big Map which encompasses them all. Recommended for the beginning mapper and nature enthusiast.

Hornblow, Leonora and Arthur, ***Birds Do the Strangest Things***, Random House, NY, 1991. A Step Up Paperback book with twenty chapters about different birds.

Jeffers, Susan, ***Brother Eagle Sister Sky,*** Dial Press, NY, 1990. This beautifully illustrated book recounts the wisdom of Chief Seattle as he learned from childhood to care for and love all of Nature as his brothers and sisters of the Earth. All things are connected, like the blood which unites one people.

Kenzie, Alice, ***"Suite for a Jumping Mouse"*** (cassette), Rabbit Recordings, Wolcott, Vermont. (Available from: Rabbit Recordings, RD2 Blush Hill, Waterbury, VT, 05676) The classic "Jumping Mouse Legend" is retold by this Vermont artist, complete with original instrumentals and a moving storytelling style. See additional details described below in Storm's book *Seven Arrows.*

Longfellow, Henry David, *Hiawatha*, Dial Press, NY, 1989. A classic poem about a young Native boy who grows with love and wonder for the Earth around him. Wonderful illustrations by Susan Jeffers.

McLerran, Alice, *The Mountain That Loved A Bird*, Picture Book Studios, MA. Illustrated by Eric Carle, this wonderful story tells of a bird which migrates past a lonely mountain all her life. The mountain pleads with her to take up residence on his rocky cliff. But, alas, the bird finds it unsuitable, until one day.... This is a great story about how one habitat evolves into another. The story lends itself to creating a student-made flannel board lesson for ecology concepts such as succession.

Paulus, Trina, *Hope for the Flowers*, Paulist Press, NJ, 1972. Two caterpillars share their life story of achievement, love, separation, faith, trust and change.

Pirtle, Sarah, "My Roots Go Down": from cassette *My Two Hands Hold the Earth,* Discovery Center, P.O. Box 28, Buckland, MA, 01338

Sattler, Helen Roney, *The Book of Eagles*, Lothrup, Lee & Shepard, NY, 1989. Illustrated information regarding the nature of eagles, hunting, courtship and nesting, baby eagles, and the relationship between eagles and the human community.

Schwartz, David M., *The Hidden Life of the Meadow*, Crown Publishing, NY, 1988. A close up look at what might go unnoticed in the world of the meadow.

Selsam, Millicent E., *Where Do They Go? Insects in Winter*, Four Winds Press, NY, 1982. Here are some answers for the curious winter naturalist.

Steptoe, John, *The Story of Jumping Mouse*, Ballantine Books, NY, 1987. A retelling of Storm's story of Jumping Mouse with a bit of a different twist. See the description below.

Storm, Hyemeyohsts, *Seven Arrows*, Ballantine Books, NY, 1972. Within this book (on page 68) you will find the original inspiring Native American story of a Jumping Mouse who does not let the details of sound or sight of everyday life go unnoticed. Although the world of the grasses is safe and has been home forever, a great longing to know the world takes Jumping Mouse on some challenging adventures. Armed with courage and determination, a greater vision unfolds for the Jumping Mouse during his quest for knowledge.

Suzuki, David, **Looking at Insects**, Warner Books, NY, 1989. Lots of great hands-on adventures with insects that kids can try themselves.

Walking Night Bear, **Song of the Seven Herbs**, Gold Circle Productions, CA, 1983. Seven stories and illustrations of the Sunflower, Wild Lettuce, Violet, Stinging Nettle, Yarrow, Dandelion, and Wild Rose are inspired by Native American tradition. Each story is told through the journey of a child learning the wisdom of the herbs.

Watts, Barrie, **Keeping Minibeasts: Ants**, Franlkin Watts Publishing, NY, 1990. A how-to book for caring for ants indoors.

White, E.B., **The Trumpet of the Swan**, Harper & Row, NY, 1970. This read-aloud chapter book tells the story of Louis, a swan without a voice. A young boy who befriends Louis takes him to school to learn to read and write. How will this help to solve Louis's larger problem when he falls in love with a beautiful swan?

Zim, Herbert, **Golden Nature Guide to Birds**, Golden Press, NY, 1956. Simple field identification color guide for children.

Zim, Herbert, **Golden Nature Guide to Flowers**, Golden Press, NY, 1950. Simple field identification color guide for children.

The following stories, poems, and guided journeys were written by JoAnne Dennee:

"Nature Names: Birch Bark Emblems"
"Nature Neighborhood Mandala"
"Plantain Heals the Pain"
"Thankyou Sister Clover Blossom"
"When Sun Spirit Sends the Sunbeams Down"
"To Be An Ant"

The following stories and poems were written by Julia Hand:

"Butterfly Tree"
"Butterfly"
"Home Again, Home Again"
"Celia's Jewels"
"Black Bear's Plan"
"Petra, the Impatient Pupa"
"Gallfly Year"
"The Story of Jumping Mouse" (adapted from oral tradition)
"Butterfly Garden"
"How the Birds Got Their Wings"
"The Gift of the Medicinal Plants"

The following story was written by Carolyn Peduzzi:

"Old Man Winter Meets Spring"